Flakes, Jugs, and Splitters

Brittany Griffith climbs Camber *(5.11),*
Cathedral Ledge, New Hampshire.
PHOTO BY JIM SURETTE

HOW TO CLIMB™ SERIES

Flakes, Jugs, and Splitters

A Rock Climber's Guide to Geology

Sarah Garlick

GUILFORD, CONNECTICUT
HELENA, MONTANA

AN IMPRINT OF THE GLOBE PEQUOT PRESS

To Jim

To buy books in quantity for corporate use
or incentives, call **(800) 962–0973**
or e-mail **premiums@GlobePequot.com.**

FALCONGUIDES®

Copyright © 2009 by Sarah Garlick

Falcon, FalconGuides, and Chockstone are registered trademarks of
Morris Book Publishing, LLC.
How to Climb and Outfit Your Mind are trademarks of Morris Book Pub-
lishing, LLC.

Photographs by:
  Jim Surette (www.granitefilms.com)
  Anne Skidmore (www.anneskidmore.com)
  Brian Post (www.brianpostphoto.com)
  Jim Thornburg (www.jimthornburg.com)
  Josh Helke (www.organicclimbing.com)
  Conrad Anker (www.conradanker.com)
Text design by Casey Shain
Illustrations by Sarah Garlick

Library of Congress Cataloging-in-Publication Data
Garlick, Sarah.
  Flakes, jugs, and splitters : a rock climber's guide to geology / Sarah Garlick.
     p. cm.
  ISBN 978-0-7627-4837-2
  1. Geology—United States—Popular works. 2. Geology—North America—
Popular works. I. Title.
  QE77.G25 2009
  550—dc22

                                                                    2008036950

Printed in China

10 9 8 7 6 5 4 3 2 1

Warning: Climbing is a dangerous sport. You can be seriously injured or die. Read the following before you use this book.

This is an instruction book about rock climbing, a sport that is inherently dangerous. Do not depend solely on information from this book for your personal safety. Your climbing safety depends on your own judgment based on competent instruction, experience, and a realistic assessment of your climbing ability.

There are no warranties, either expressed or implied, that this instruction book contains accurate and reliable information. There are no warranties as to fitness for a particular purpose or that this book is merchantable. Your use of this book indicates your assumption of the risk of death or serious injury as a result of climbing's risks and is an acknowledgment of your own sole responsibility for your safety in climbing or in training for climbing.

The Globe Pequot Press and the author assume no liability for accidents happening to, or injuries sustained by, readers who engage in the activities described in this book.

Kirsten Kremer crosses the glacial outwash stream on her way into the Cerro Torre group in Patagonia.

PHOTO BY SARAH GARLICK

Contents

Preface

We climb granite domes and sandstone towers, basalt bluffs and limestone caves. We pull on smooth pockets, jam splitter cracks, and crimp tiny edges. We read the rock, figuring out how to scale its features and protect its weaknesses. But why are the rocks there in the first place? How did their features form? Why are some climbing areas unique and others so similar? This book is your guide to the geology of the world's most popular climbing destinations. Region by region, *Flakes, Jugs, and Splitters* ticks off answers to all your rock questions.

Flakes, Jugs, and Splitters is primarily focused on rock climbing areas in North America, especially in the United States. Whole separate volumes could be written about the climbing areas in Europe, Asia, Africa, South America, and Australia—and hopefully they will be. Within the scope of this book, however, only a few highlights of these destinations are presented.

Flakes, Jugs, and Splitters is organized with an introductory Geology 101 section that will get you up to speed with basic geologic concepts that are helpful for understanding the topics covered in the rest of the book. From there, chapters explore the geology of individual geographic regions in a question-and-answer format. The General Rock Questions chapter at the end of this book covers topics that aren't restricted to a specific area: for example, why sandstone is sometimes red and sometimes white and how boulders form. Flip through the Q-and-A chapters at your leisure or read the book straight through. If there is a particular location or topic you're interested in, try the index in the back.

The information within this book was compiled primarily from research papers in peer-reviewed scientific journals. Other sources include science guidebooks, climbing guidebooks, textbooks, and interviews with scientists. A complete list of references can be found in the back of the book. Numbers corresponding to specific sources are listed at the end of each topic.

Acknowledgments

This book would not be possible without the staff and supporters of the University of Wyoming Brinkerhoff Geology Library, which houses one of the finest collections of Earth science publications in the country. I would like to thank my geology teachers, especially Art Snoke from the University of Wyoming and Jan Tullis from Brown University. I would also like to thank the talented photographers who generously contributed to this book: Jim Surette, Brian Post, Anne Skidmore, Jim Thornburg, Josh Helke, Majka Burhardt, Rachael Lynn, Kirsten Kremer, John Burbidge, Conrad Anker, and Gordon Medaris Jr. Technical reviews by Dr. B. R. Frost, Dr. Arthur W. Snoke, and Dr. Elizabeth A. Hajek contributed to the quality of this book, but any errors or omissions are my own. I would like to extend special thanks to climber-geologist Liz Hajek and to Josh Helke for their brainstorming sessions and advice. Also, my gratitude and apologies go to my climbing partners, with whom I had to break many climbing dates to finish this book. Finally, and most importantly, I thank Jim Surette and the members of my family for their love and support.

*Mark Synnott, Jared Ogden, and
Alex Lowe hike beneath spires
made up of 21-million-year-old
granite in Pakistan.*
PHOTO BY JIM SURETTE

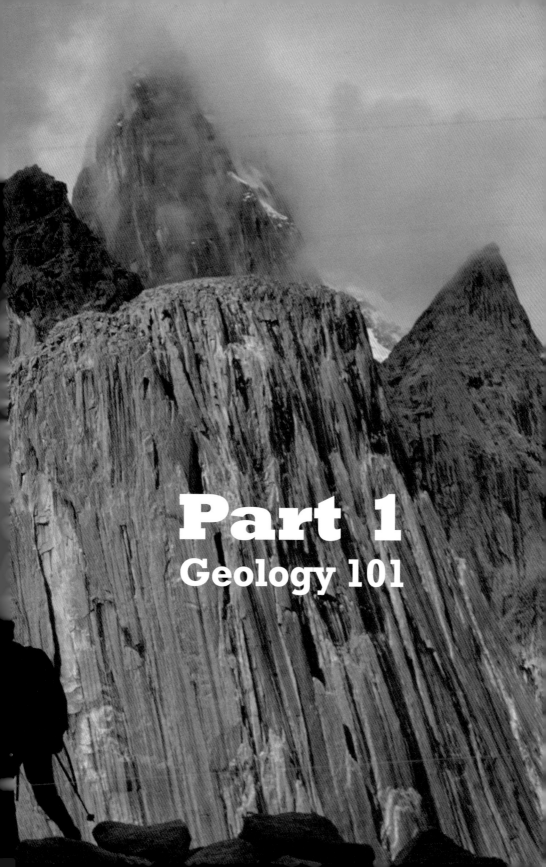

Part 1
Geology 101

Eric Candee latching onto a limestone jug in Glenwood Canyon, Colorado.
PHOTO BY JIM SURETTE

The Basics

Geology is the study of the Earth: how it is constructed, how it is changing, how it has changed in the past. It is an overarching field that encompasses many subdisciplines and topics. At its basic level, however, geology is a study of processes: of how landforms are sculpted, how mountains are uplifted, how rocks are created and then destroyed, and how environments—global and local—have changed through time. There are rarely single answers to geologic questions: that one cause corresponds with one effect, for example. Instead, the Earth is shaped by an interplay of different processes, some simple and some complex, each of which operates on its own scale and time frame. It can make your head spin at first, but once you understand a few of the most important processes and their outcomes, you will look at the rocks and mountains you climb in a different light, one that reflects the richness of the history of the land and the sometimes unbelievable power of our truly dynamic planet. In this chapter I present five of the most important Earth processes, the concepts of which are repeated over and over again in the rest of the book. Before I get to these processes, however, two integral pieces of groundwork must be laid: the concept of geologic time and the theory of plate tectonics.

Millions and Billions: The Grand Scale of Geologic Time

The concept of geologic time is not an easy one to immediately grasp. How can someone really understand the meaning of a hundred million years or a billion years when that amount of time can't be experienced directly? How do geologists talk about millions and billions of years as easily as the rest of us talk about weeks and months? The key is to put the big numbers of geologic time into a context of a sequence of events. The more events you come to understand and mentally organize, the more familiar and useful the grand scale of geologic time becomes.

One way to begin is to structure the timescale with a history we all relate to: the history of life. The earliest evidence for life on Earth is 3.5 billion years old, which is about a billion years after the formation of our planet. The oxygen atmosphere we enjoy today started to develop 2.2 billion years ago (before that it was mostly carbon dioxide). Animals didn't invade the land until about 420 million years ago, and the earliest humans (hominids) appeared about 5 million years ago.

Figure 1 is a chart that depicts the geologic timescale labeled with important events relevant to climbers. Ordovician, Carboniferous, Cretaceous: The names on the timescale may seem like jargon at first, but they are helpful for categorizing the relative ages of rocks as well as for talking about events that took place over long periods of time. This book uses the names of periods and epochs as well as direct dates in millions of years to give you several reference points for comparing the geologic histories of different climbing areas. Sometimes the exact age of a rock or land formation is well established—the El Capitan granite, for example, is 102 million years old. Other times, all that is known is a general or estimated age—for example, the Corbin sandstone at the Red River Gorge is Pennsylvanian in age, which means it was deposited sometime between about 318 and 299 million years ago.

How do geologists know that the El Capitan granite is 102 million years old rather than, say, 103 million years old? By the same token, why can't they figure out exactly how old the sandstone is at the Red River Gorge? The science of determining the ages of rocks and landforms is called geochronology, and it has advanced to the point where some geologic materials can be dated with incredible precision. The secret to this type of geochronology is a group of elements that are found within the minerals of some common rocks. These elements act as tiny clocks, recording the passage of time by their radioactive decay. Radioactive decay occurs at a known rate, so by measuring the amount of the starting material, called the parent, and the amount of the material into which the starting material decays, called the daughter, scientists use the known decay rate to calculate how long the material has been in existence. One of the most important of these geologic clocks is uranium, which decays into lead over a long time period, making it useful for determining the ages of rocks that are hundreds of millions and even billions of years old. Uranium is abundant in the mineral zircon, which is a common component in igneous rocks like granite.

Another important geochronological tool is called relative age dating. This is a technique of sequencing the relative age of rocks without necessarily knowing a direct date. For example, we know that sedimentary rocks are deposited horizontally, so by looking at an undisturbed sequence of sedimentary rocks, one can determine that the lower layers are older than the upper layers. Crosscutting bodies relate to a relative sequence because they must be younger than the rocks that they cross. Often sedimentary rocks that cannot be directly dated by radiometric tools can be estimated by the direct date of a crosscutting igneous dike, and/or the age range of fossils found within the sedimentary layers.

Earth as a Jigsaw Puzzle: Plate Tectonics

Everything about the Earth that we most enjoy as climbers—the mountains, the crags, and the boulders—at a fundamental level, they all exist because of plate tectonics. It may sound overly technical at first, but plate tectonics is just a fancy title for the movements that occur in Earth's crust. These are the movements that cause mountains to rise and volcanoes to erupt. They cause basins to subside and fill with sediment; and they are responsible for the uplift of deep rocks like granite to become exposed at the Earth's surface.

Technically speaking, plate tectonic movements affect the lithosphere, which includes the Earth's crust as well as the very upper portion of its mantle (see figure 2). The lithosphere is the rigid, outermost shell of the planet ("litho" means rock in Greek), and it is broken up into a mosaic of different plates. As these plates move, sliding around on the hotter, weaker rocks below, they influence the shape and nature of the planet's surface upon which we live and climb.

The important thing to know about plate tectonics is that most of the action takes place along the boundaries of the plates, where adjacent plates meet. Specific plate tectonic environments are created by the type of movement along these boundaries, which, in turn, create specific features like volcanoes, mountain chains, and earthquakes. There are three main types of plate tectonic boundaries: convergent, divergent, and transform (see figure 3).

FIGURE 1

A Climber's View of Geologic Time

Note: Ages are listed in millions of years before present (Ma) and reflect the approximate age of the rock itself, not the landform in which the rock is exposed.

Era	Period/Eon/Epoch	Approximate Ages of Rocks
PALEOZOIC	**Precambrian eon** (4540–542 Ma)	Gallatin Canyon, Montana: gneiss (3500–3300 Ma) Big Horn Mountains, Wyoming: granodiorite (2800 Ma) Cirque of the Towers, Wyoming: granite (2600 Ma) Grand Teton, Wyoming: quartz monzonite (2500 Ma) Oxygen atmosphere develops (2200 Ma) Baffin Island: granitic rocks (1800 Ma) Devils Lake, Wisconsin: Baraboo quartzite (1750–1630 Ma) The Needles, South Dakota: granite (1700 Ma) Black Canyon of the Gunnison, Colorado: granitic rocks 　　(1700 Ma & 1400 Ma) Mount Lemmon, Arizona: Oracle granite (1400 Ma) The Diamond/Longs Peak, Colorado: Silver Plume granite 　　(1400 Ma) Vedauwoo, Wyoming: Sherman granite (1400 Ma) Taylors Falls, Minnesota & Wisconsin: basalt (1100 Ma)
	Cambrian period (542–488 Ma)	Linville Gorge, North Carolina: quartzite Moore's Wall, North Carolina: quartzite
	Ordovician period (488–444 Ma)	Buffalo River, Arizona: sedimentary rocks Whiteside Mountain, North Carolina: tonalite (465 Ma) Sinks Canyon, Wyoming: Bighorn Dolomite Wild Iris, Wyoming: Bighorn Dolomite Rocklands/Table Mountain, South Africa: sandstone Mount Everest: Yellow Band metamorphosed limestone
	Silurian period (444–416 Ma)	Animals reach land Rumney, New Hampshire: Littleton Formation Shawangunk Mountains, New York: Shawangunk 　　Conglomerate Seneca Rocks, West Virginia: Tuscarora Formation Rocklands/Table Mountain, South Africa: sandstone Grampians, Australia: sandstone
	Devonian period (416–359 Ma)	Acadia National Park, Maine: Cadillac granite Looking Glass, North Carolina: granodiorite
	Carboniferous period **Mississippian epoch** (359–318 Ma)	Rifle, Colorado: Leadville limestone
	Carboniferous period **Pennsylvanian epoch** (318–299 Ma)	New River Gorge, West Virginia: Nutall sandstone Red River Gorge, Kentucky: Corbin sandstone Tennessee Wall, Tennessee: Gizzard Group sandstone Horse Pens 40, Alabama: Pottsville Formation sandstone Sam's Throne, Arkansas: Atoka Sandstone Peak Disrict, England: Millstone grit
	Permian period (299–251 Ma)	Eldorado Canyon, Colorado: Fountain Formation Flatirons, Colorado: Fountain Formation Garden of the Gods, Colorado: Fountain Formation Fisher Towers, Utah: Cutler Formation Railay Beach, Thailand: Ratburi Group limestone

MESOZOIC		
Triassic period (251–200 Ma)	Indian Creek, Utah: Wingate Formation (late Triassic/early Jurassic) Castleton Tower, Utah: Wingate Formation
Jurassic period (200–146 Ma)	Indian Creek, Utah: Wingate Formation Castleton Tower, Utah: Wingate Formation Zion, Utah: Aztec Sandstone Cathedral Ledge, New Hampshire: Conway granite Red Rocks, Nevada: Aztec Sandstone The Eiger, Switzerland: limestone
Cretaceous period (146–66 Ma)	Yosemite, California: El Capitan granite (102 Ma) Tuolumne, California: Tuolumne Intrusive Suite Bishop, California: Buttermilk boulders: Sierra Nevada Batholith Joshua Tree, California: White Tank monzogranite Bugaboos, Canada: Bugaboo Batholith Maple Canyon, Utah: Price River Formation conglomerate Europe: limestone

CENOZOIC		
Paleocene epoch (66–56 Ma)	Alaska Range, Alaska: granitic rock
Eocene epoch (56–34 Ma)	Mount Lemmon, Arizona: Wilderness granite (50 Ma) Devils Tower, Wyoming; phonolite (40 Ma) Hueco Tanks, Texas: syenite porphyry (34 Ma) Little Cottonwood Canyon, Utah: Little Cottonwood stock (37–30 Ma)
Oligocene epoch (34–23 Ma)	Little Cottonwood Canyon, Utah: Little Cottonwood stock (37–30 Ma) City of Rocks, Idaho: Alamo pluton (29 Ma) Smith Rock, Oregon: welded tuff and rhyolite (30 Ma) Mount Lemmon, Arizona: Catalina monzogranite (26 Ma) Castle Hill, New Zealand: Canterbury Basin limestone Fontainebleau, France: Fontainebleau sandstone Cochise Stronghold, Arizona: Stronghold granite (28–22 Ma) Shiprock, New Mexico: Navajo volcanic field (30–20 Ma)
Miocene epoch (23–5.3 Ma)	Great Trango Tower, Pakistan: Baltoro granite (21 Ma) Fitz Roy & Cerro Torre, Argentina: Fitz Roy pluton (18 Ma) Torres del Paine, Chile: granitic rock (18 Ma) Cordillera Blanca, Peru: Cordillera Blanca Batholith granodiorite (8 Ma)
Pliocene epoch (5.3–1.8 Ma)	First humans (5 Ma)
Pleistocene epoch (1.8 Ma–11,500 years ago)	Bishop, California: Happy and Sad boulders: Bishop Tuff Owens River Gorge, California: Bishop Tuff Last Ice Age
Recent (11,500 years ago–present)	

FIGURE 2

A

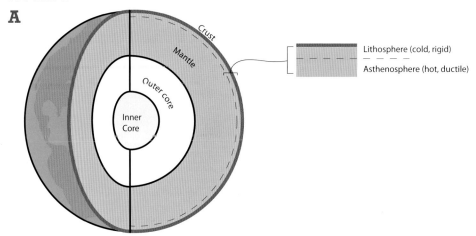

Lithosphere (cold, rigid)
Asthenosphere (hot, ductile)

A. The Earth is compositionally layered, with a silica-rich outer crust; a magnesium- and iron-rich mantle; and an iron core, subdivided into a liquid outer core and a solid inner core. The Earth's crust varies in thickness from 3 to 5 miles beneath the oceans to an average of 20 miles beneath the continents. Continental crust, however, can reach over 60 miles in thickness in large mountain ranges and be less than 3 miles thick in areas of rifting. At about 1,800 miles, the mantle is Earth's thickest compositional layer. The liquid outer core is about 1,100 miles thick, while the solid inner core is almost half that—750 miles thick.

B

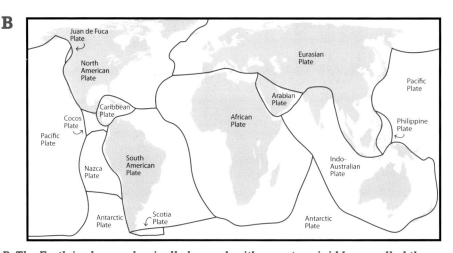

B. The Earth is also mechanically layered, with an outer, rigid layer called the lithosphere and an underlying, weaker layer called the asthenosphere. The lithosphere is broken into a mosaic of tectonic plates that move around the planet like rafts on top of the asthenosphere.

Convergent boundaries occur when two adjacent plates converge, or move toward each other. If the crust of one plate is denser than the other, as is the case between oceanic and continental crust, the denser material will slide beneath the more buoyant material along a trench. This process is called subduction. Volcanoes and large mountain chains of folded sedimentary rock form in the upper plate of subduction zones due to the compressional forces along this type of tectonic boundary and the magma that is generated by the heating of the downgoing plate.

A modern example of this tectonic boundary is the western margin of South America, where oceanic crust is subducting downward to the east beneath the continent, resulting in the formation of the Andean mountain chain. Another result of a convergent boundary is a continental collision zone. If two convergent plates have relatively equal buoyancy, as is the case between two continental plates, the crust between them will buckle and shorten, thrusting up a huge continental collision zone of mountains. The best modern example of this tectonic environment is the Himalayan mountain chain, which is thrust up between the colliding continent of Asia and subcontinent of India.

The second type of plate tectonic boundary is divergent. Divergent boundaries occur when two plates move away from each other, separating along a feature called a spreading center. Spreading centers are found along the central axis of most oceans, where they are called mid-ocean ridges, and they are where most new oceanic crust is made. Along these divergent boundaries, the two adjacent tectonic plates move away from each other as if riding on oppositely oriented conveyor belts. In the space created by the diverging plates, magma rises up from the mantle and then cools, forming new basaltic ocean crust. The crust along divergent boundaries is thus usually very thin, young, and relatively hot. As you move perpendicularly away from the mid-ocean ridge, the ocean crust becomes thicker, older, and cooler.

The third type of the Earth's plate tectonic boundaries, called transform boundaries, occurs when two adjacent plates move laterally along side each other. Instead of moving directly toward or away from the boundary, the plates slide past each other, grinding along a vertical fault zone. One of the best modern examples of a transform boundary is the San Andreas Fault in California, where the Pacific Plate slides northward past the North America Plate. Small bends in transform boundaries can cause local convergent or

FIGURE 3

Types of Tectonic Boundaries

A.

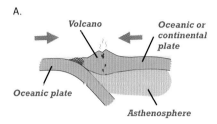

A. Convergent boundary: subduction zone
Where two tectonic plates converge, the denser plate dives down beneath the more buoyant plate along an oceanic trench. Fluids are driven off the downgoing plate, facilitating melting of the underlying asthenosphere. The magma rises into the upper plate, eventually reaching the Earth's surface as volcanoes.

B.

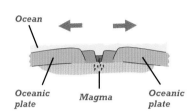

B. Divergent boundary: mid-ocean ridge
Divergent boundaries, where plates move away from each other, are called rift zones or spreading centers. New oceanic crust is produced by magma upwelling along these boundaries.

C. Convergent boundary: continent-continent collision
When two continental plates converge, they are too buoyant to subduct and thus crash into each other in a continent-continent collision. These collisions produce large mountain chains and ultra-thick continental crust.

C.

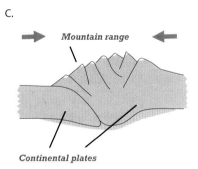

D. Transform boundary
In addition to convergent and divergent boundaries, two tectonic plates can slide past each other along a transform boundary, which is essentially a large strike-slip fault. There are many transform boundaries in the oceans, separating different segments of oceanic spreading centers. There are also continental transform boundaries, like the San Andreas Fault in California.

D.

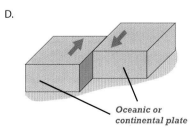

divergent motion, but the overall tectonic environment of transform boundaries is strike-slip, or alongside fault motion.

The three types of tectonic boundaries—convergent, divergent, and transform—can occur along different sections of the same plate edge. For example, the Pacific Ocean–North American continent boundary in Alaska is primarily convergent (there is a subduction zone beneath the Aleutian Islands), whereas it is transform along most of California.

Plate tectonics as a whole is an elegant theory that unifies nearly every aspect of the physical Earth and represents the framework by which we view and understand our planet. Despite its influences, however, the theory of plate tectonics is still relatively young and has only gained wide acceptance in the scientific community in the past thirty years. This means that there are many big, fundamental questions to still be answered about how the world works. Some of the questions geologists are tackling right now include: When and why did plate tectonics begin? What exactly drives plate tectonics? What are the mechanisms by which the continents have grown? What is the expected evolutionary track of large mountain chains? How exactly are deep rocks uplifted to the Earth's surface? As you will find in the rest of this book, these topics relate to many of the world's climbing areas. Perhaps in the future we will find that some of their answers are hidden away at these areas as well.

Devils Tower is made up of phonolite,
an uncommon extrusive igneous rock.
PHOTO BY RACHAEL LYNN

Five Important Earth Processes

Liquid, Hot Magma: The Formation of Igneous Rocks

Unless you climb exclusively in the desert, it's likely that you'll have many of your climbing adventures on and around igneous rocks like granite and basalt. So one of the most important large-scale Earth processes to affect climbers is the formation of this rock type. Igneous rocks, by definition, are rocks that originate as magma, or molten rock. The basic process of their formation involves two stages: the generation of the magma and then the cooling or quenching of that magma into solid rock. The variations and intricacies of these two stages lead to the different types of igneous rocks found on Earth. Where and how the magma is generated controls the chemistry and type of the final rock, and the environment and amount of time in which the magma is cooled determines the texture of that rock.

There are two general types of igneous rocks: intrusive and extrusive. Intrusive igneous rocks are rocks that cool within the Earth's crust as plutons, dikes, sills, and batholiths, emplaced within preexisting rock (see figure 31). Extrusive rocks, on the other hand, are rocks that are extruded or erupted onto the Earth's surface, where they cool from lava flows. Intrusive rocks are also called plutonic or magmatic rocks, and they include the granite family (see below), as well as diorite and gabbro. Extrusive rocks are known as volcanic rocks, and they include basalt and rhyolite. One of the main differences between intrusive and extrusive rocks is their texture. Intrusive rocks are slowly cooled and thus are coarse grained; you can pick out individual crystals with your naked eye, and these crystals fit together

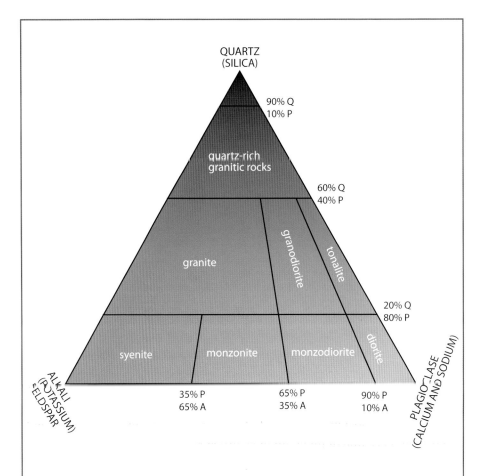

FIGURE 4

Triangle Diagram of Igneous Rock Classification

The triangle shows rock types based on their relative compositions of quartz, plagioclase, and alkali feldspar. Each tip of the triangle corresponds to a composition that is 100% the mineral shown. For example, a quartz vein made up of 100% quartz would lie on the top "quartz" tip of the triangle. Furthermore, a rock with equal amounts of quartz, alkali feldspar, and plagioclase would lie in the dead center of the triangle, within the "granite" field.

This is a generalized diagram; geologists subdivide these compositional fields even more than is shown. For example, geologists will call a rock a quartz monzonite if it is closer to the border between "granite" and "monzonite" (i.e., more quartz). They will call a rock a monzogranite if it is in the "granite" field but close to the "monzonite" border.

Taken for Granite

The single-line entry in the geology section of an early climbing guide to New Hampshire echoes the opinion of many climbers: "Granite. Amen." But what is granite exactly? Why do people call the rock in Yosemite "granite" but the rock in Joshua Tree "quartz monzonite" and "monzogranite"? The ambiguity over the word "granite" has trickled down from geologists, who have come up with so many different classification schemes for igneous rocks that a simple definition can be hard to come by. A broadly acceptable definition is that granite is an intrusive igneous rock made up of quartz, potassium feldspar, plagioclase, and usually an iron-magnesium mineral like hornblende or biotite. The relative amounts of quartz, plagioclase, and potassium feldspar determine if the rock is a true granite or if it is a related "granitic" rock like a granodiorite or a monzonite. The diagram in figure 4 depicts a commonly used classification scheme showing the relationships between these different igneous intrusive rocks. Granitic rocks may have a slight visible fabric, or alignment of minerals, caused by currents in the magma chamber as the rock cooled. If a rock looks similar to a granite but has a strong, through-going alignment of minerals in a layering pattern, it is probably a granitic gneiss—a metamorphic rock that once was a granite but then was heated and squished into its new form.

in a visible, interlocking network. Extrusive rocks are rapidly quenched and are usually very fine grained, often so much so that you can only pick out individual crystals with a high-powered microscope. Extrusive igneous rocks may have inclusions or clasts brought up through the volcano during eruption, or many small holes or pockets where gasses escaped.

The compositions of igneous rocks can be linked to their tectonic environment. Along divergent plate boundaries like midoceanic ridges, hot rocks from the mantle rise up toward the ridge by convection currents; as they depressurize they partially melt, forming basaltic magma. This magma erupts along the ocean floor and cools in the shallow regions of the Earth, creating basaltic oceanic crust. Similarly, in regions of very thin crust, like rift basins along the Rio Grande Rift in New Mexico, magma generated in the upper mantle can penetrate the crust and the volcanism tends to be basaltic. Along convergent boundaries, however, the Earth's crust is thickened; crustal rocks as well as mantle rocks melt in these environments. These magmas are richer in silica than basalts, resulting in the granites and granodiorites that are common in subduction and collisional zones.

Coral Reefs, Beach Sand, and Dirt: The Formation of Sedimentary Rocks

Another large-scale Earth process important to climbers is the formation of sedimentary rocks. Without sedimentary rocks, there would be no Indian Creek or Rifle, no Red River Gorge or sport crags in Europe. Rocks that belong to the sedimentary group include limestone, sandstone, shale, conglomerate, and even volcanic tuff. These are all sedimentary rocks because they formed by the accumulation and consolidation of loose particles. These particles, or sediments, were either transported and then deposited or were precipitated in place out of solution.

Most sedimentary rocks can be classified as terrigenous (meaning "of the land") clastic rocks, volcaniclastic rocks, or carbonate rocks. Terrigenous clastic rocks are rocks derived from particles ("clasts") that are eroded from pre-existing bedrock. Terrigenous clastic rocks include sandstones, mudstones, and conglomerates. Volcaniclastic rocks are rocks that form from the accumulation of volcanic material, usually hot ash that was spewed into the atmosphere during eruption and then deposited on the land surface in a thick blanket. Carbonate rocks are limestones, which by definition are composed of over 50 percent calcium carbonate. The shells and bones of many marine animals are made up of calcium carbonate; thus most limestones are marine in origin.

Just as the chemistry and texture of igneous rocks record the deep, interior environments in the crust, the composition and texture of sedimentary rocks record the exterior environment of the Earth's surface. With the exception of salt deposits and some carbonate rocks that form from direct precipitation out of solution, the particles or grains in sedimentary rocks are involved in some sort of physical transport in a specific environment on the surface of the Earth. For example, sandstones can be deposited by wind action in giant dune fields, by water current action along rivers, or by wave and current action in shallow marine waters along a beach shoreline. The size of the particles in these rocks is a clue to its depositional environment. The coarser the grain, the higher energy the environment had to be. Very coarse sedimentary rocks like conglomerates require high-energy deposition like landslides, floods, or glaciers to transport the big particles. Very fine sedimentary rocks like mudstones and shales are deposited in very low-energy environments like deep, calm lakes or the deep waters of oceans. Medium-grained sediment like sands can be deposited in windblown sand dunes, beaches, or rivers.

The compositional makeup of sediments in sedimentary rocks is also important to determining the past environments in which the rocks were formed. The more a sediment is worked by its environment, by energy or by time, the more the sediment becomes physically and chemically broken down, thus controlling the composition of the final sedimentary rock. The first components to become broken down during transport and time are the iron and magnesium minerals like micas and amphiboles, and then the calcium, aluminum, and potassium minerals like feldspars. Silica is the last component to be worn away, so a sediment that is far traveled from its source will be mostly made up of quartz (which is composed of silica and oxygen). Marine environments, on the other hand, are usually indicated by the presence of calcium carbonate rather than terrigenous materials like quartz and feldspars. Calcium carbonate exists in marine rocks in the form of limey muds, shell and bone fragments, or as minerals directly precipitated out of saturated seawater.

The compositional and textural environmental indicators in sedimentary rocks are important because they allow us to read environmental changes on the Earth through time. For example, if you have a sequence of clastic sedimentary rocks that shows a coarsening of grain size (e.g., shale to fine-grained sandstone to coarse-grained sandstone), then you can infer that the energy of the depositional environment increased with time. One way this happens is by a drop in sea level. The shale is deposited in the quiet waters of a deep ocean. As sea level drops and the deep-ocean environment becomes a shallow-ocean environment, coarser sands are deposited. Finally, when sea level drops even more, the environment becomes a beach, where even coarser sands exist.

Other environmental factors you can read in sedimentary rocks are the location of mountains. Basins develop adjacent to mountain ranges and they fill with sediment. Usually the first rocks to be shed in the basins are coarse conglomerates that reflect debris flows off the high mountains. As the mountains are worn down, lower energy environments like rivers carry the sediment into the basin, and sandstones are deposited.

In order to turn a pile of sediment into sedimentary rock, the sediment has to go through a process called lithification. Lithification is the compaction and solidification of sediments into a coherent rock, usually by both physical and chemical processes. Turning a sediment into a rock can happen many different ways and on different timescales—as quickly as the sediment is deposited or as slowly as millions of years. Most sediment, however, requires burial to become sedimentary rock. As sediment deposits become progressively buried, their temperatures and pressures increase, facilitating the chemical and physical changes of lithification.

One of these changes is the development of a cement, which is essentially the "glue" that holds sedimentary rocks together. Common cements are made up of silica dissolved from quartz, and calcium carbonate coming from calcite. These cements form when fluids moving through the pore space of compacted sediments precipitate the chemicals they are carrying. Iron-rich cements can also form; these commonly occur by the breakdown of volcanic or igneous fragments in a rock.

Heating and Squeezing: The Formation of Metamorphic Rocks

Metamorphic rocks are the third major rock type on Earth. "Meta" means "change"; thus metamorphic rocks are igneous or sedimentary rocks that have been physically and chemically changed, usually by heating and/or squeezing in an active tectonic environment. The most common metamorphic rocks climbers encounter are gneiss, schist, and quartzite. These rocks are easily identified by features that can be seen with your eye. Gneisses are hard crystalline rocks, similar to intrusive igneous rocks but with a distinctive layering that gives the rock a banded appearance. Schists are also layered metamorphic rocks, but they have much finer layers, almost like thin flakes, that are created by alignments of mica. In general, gneisses tend to form out of coarse-grained igneous and sedimentary rocks, whereas schists typically form out of finer grained rocks, especially sedimentary rocks that originally had a significant component of fine clay minerals. These fine clay minerals are what alter into the platy micas during metamorphism. Quartzite is a special type of metamorphic rock because it is almost entirely composed of the mineral quartz. Quartzites typically form by the metamorphism of relatively pure quartz sandstones. During metamorphism, the quartz grains weld together, creating one of the hardest rocks on the planet.

Because metamorphic rocks have this history as being different rock types—some gneisses were once granites, for example—geologists that are interested in past Earth conditions will often times refer to metamorphic rocks by their original names. For example, you might find some quartzites described as sandstones, although technically they are meta-sandstones.

The temperatures and pressures required to change a rock enough that it becomes a metamorphic rock can occur in several different settings. One simple way is to heat rocks by flooding the crust with hot magma, which occurs during the intrusion of large plutons. This sudden burst of heat can change the surrounding rocks of the plutons in a process called contact metamorphism. The other type of metamorphism, called regional metamorphism, occurs when a body of rock is subjected to elevated pressures and temperatures either by burial, subduction, or tectonic collision.

Faulting, Folding, and Rock Uplift: The Making of Mountains

For climbers, the formation of igneous, sedimentary, and metamorphic rocks does little good if the rocks aren't exposed as cliffs, mountains, and boulders on the Earth's surface. Therefore, in order to understand the geology of different climbing areas, one must understand how the landforms of those climbing areas were created. All landforms, be they mountains, plateaus, gorges, or valleys, are the result of a competition that exists between the forces that build up the land and the forces that tear the land down. This section covers the forces that build up the land; the final section in this chapter discusses the forces that tear the land down.

Rocks can be uplifted into highlands like scarps, cliffs, and mountains by several different processes, including volcanism, folding, and faulting. These processes are all components of what geologists call orogenesis, which simply means mountain building ("oro" is Greek for "mountain"). In geologic history, mountain-building events are called orogenies.

Rocks can be uplifted by the development of large folds. Folds usually occur in sedimentary rocks, which are weaker and more easily deformed than crystalline rocks, and they develop by compressional forces that cause contraction in the crust. Contraction occurs in the upper plate of a subduction zone as well as in both plates of a collisional zone. Folding during orogenesis usually occurs in concert with faulting.

Faults are defined as fracture planes along which rocks move. Rocks are uplifted along faults and buried along them; sometimes they stay in the same vertical position but are translated horizontally along faults. These

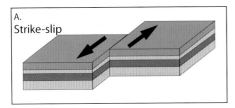

A.
Strike-slip

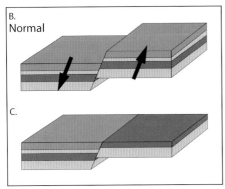

B.
Normal

C.

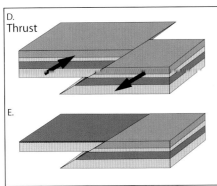

D.
Thrust

E.

FIGURE 5

Three Types of Faults

A. **Strike-slip faults are the plane along which rocks slide past each other and there is little or no vertical movement.**

B. **Normal faults are steep planes along which rocks above the fault plane slide down relative to rocks below the fault plane.**

C. **After erosion along a normal fault, young rock layers are juxtaposed with old rock layers in a young-over-old relationship.**

D. **Thrust faults are relatively shallow planes along which rocks above the fault plane slide up and over rocks below the fault plane.**

E. **After erosion along a thrust fault, old rock layers are juxtaposed with young rock layers in an old-over-young relationship.**

three types of movement correspond to the three main types of faults: thrust faults, normal faults, and strike-slip faults.

Thrust faults develop during contraction in the crust, usually when there is shortening and folding along a tectonic boundary, like in a continent-continent collision or a subduction zone. Thrust faults are defined as planes upon which deeper, older rocks are pushed up over shallower, younger rocks (see figure 5). Thrust faults typically lie at relatively low angles to the surface of the Earth, about 30 degrees, and they can result in the sliding and stacking together of large ramps of rock, which are called fold and thrust belts. Steeper thrust faults (60 to 80 degrees) also exist, and these are called reverse faults. The uplift of many of the Rocky Mountains in Colorado and Wyoming occurred along deep-seated reverse faults.

A normal fault is a fault that brings shallow, young rocks over the tops of deeper, older rocks (see figure 5). These faults are typically found in steep angles, 60 to 80 degrees, and they develop where there is extension in the crust, usually due to rifting in a plate or divergence along the tectonic margins of adjacent plates. The Rio Grande Rift in New Mexico and the Basin and Range Province of the western United States are examples of normal faulting in extensional environments.

The third type of fault, strike-slip, are nearly vertical faults (90 degrees) that have transform motion, meaning one side of the fault slides past the other side. One of the most famous strike-slip faults is the San Andreas Fault in California, where the western side of the fault is moving northward relative to the eastern side. Large-scale strike-slip faults like the San Andreas will locally develop zones of extension and contraction if there are bends in the fault plane. The Southern Alps of New Zealand are thrust up along the Alpine Fault, which is a transform boundary with mostly strike-slip motion. A bend in the fault, however, has caused local contraction and thrusting, resulting in the uplift of mountains.

Sculptures of Wind and Water: Erosion and Weathering

The forces that tear down the highlands that are created during orogenesis are the processes of erosion and weathering. Erosion and weathering together refine and shape the Earth's surface into all of its spectacular landforms.

Although they sound similar, erosion and weathering are not the same thing. Weathering refers to the processes that loosen or dissolve particles of a rock, while erosion refers to the transport of those particles away from their source. Working together, processes of weathering and erosion can relatively quickly (geologically speaking) cut a mountain chain down to gently rolling hills.

Weathering comes in two flavors: physical and chemical. Physical weathering is the abrasion of a rock—wearing it down into finer particles, usually by wind, water, or ice. Chemical weathering, on the other hand, is the dissolution of rock components, usually aided by a fluid like groundwater. Chemical weathering is overall a more effective process than physical weathering, but only if conditions are conducive to dissolution. Chemical

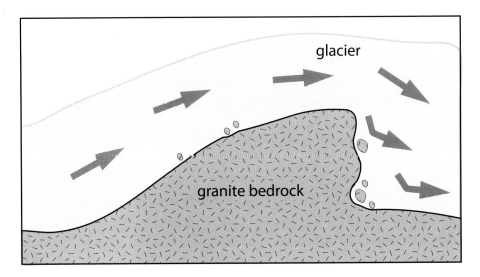

FIGURE 6
Roche moutonnée is a mountain shape formed by the advance of an ice sheet or glacier. Roche moutonnée is characteristically smooth on one side, where the glacier polished the gentle slope of the bedrock. The mountain is steep and jagged on the other side, where the glacier flowed down across a mound of bedrock, scouring and plucking boulders from its face.

weathering is accelerated by warm, humid conditions. Physical weathering is more effective in cold, windy conditions, where loosened particles can be rubbed against the rock by winds or ice. Thus physical weathering processes shape arctic and alpine regions, whereas chemical weathering processes shape landforms at lower elevations and latitudes.

Weathering processes are enhanced and aided by the work of the erosive agents: wind, water, and ice. To climbers, erosion by ice, in the form of glaciers, is one of the most important processes in shaping the landforms we enjoy. Glaciers have scoured and carved steep rock faces in many of the world's mountains, like the iconic buttresses of the Matterhorn and the sheer face of Half Dome. Glaciers are also responsible for the formation of mountain shapes called roche moutonnée (French for "rock sheep"), which are characterized by a steep cliff face on one side and a gentle slope on the other. These forms developed by the scraping motion of glaciers as they advanced (see figure 6). The Cathedral and Whitehorse ledges in New Hampshire, the hills of Acadia National Park in Maine, and many of the domes in the Sierra Nevada are examples of roche moutonnée.

Ice is a powerful erosive agent even in its more modest forms. Freeze-thaw cycles in alpine regions dramatically shape landscapes by the successive increase in volume that occurs when groundwater freezes. This can open cracks and fractures, allowing for large blocks to fall off cliff faces. The reason there tends to be more loose rock and choss in alpine environments versus lower elevation places like Yosemite Valley is the ongoing erosion of freeze-thaw cycles.

River erosion is also a key process in the development of climbing areas. Rivers have carved deep gorges throughout the globe that are enjoyed by climbers. These include the Red River Gorge, the New River Gorge, the Owen's River Gorge, and the Black Canyon of the Gunnison.

*Dana Drummond climbs Tourist Treat
(5.12+) on the 180-million-year-old Conway
Granite at Cathedral Ledge, New Hampshire.*
PHOTO BY JIM SURETTE

Part 2
Answers to All Your Rock Questions

Jeremy Johnson cranks
Man Overboard (5.12d)
on the Littleton schist in
Rumney, New Hampshire.
PHOTO BY ANNE SKIDMORE

Northeast

Why is Rumney so different from Cathedral and Whitehorse?

Despite what you might have heard, the differences between New Hampshire's sport mecca Rumney and the trad crags of North Conway have more to do with geology than with bolts. Rumney's overhanging walls and credit-card crimper holds are carved out of a ~400-million-year-old metamorphic rock called the Littleton schist. The multipitch crack and slab routes of North Conway, on the other hand, were born nearly 200 million years later when the Conway granite solidified from magma, deep in the Earth's crust.

The differences between the two climbing areas are almost entirely controlled by this difference in rock type. Schist is a type of metamorphic rock that is characterized by a fine layering of minerals—mostly micas—called a foliation. When a cliff's surface is oriented parallel to the foliation in the rock, the walls are smooth, almost featureless, with small crimpers developed where the cliff face cuts into deeper layers. The 5.14 routes at Rumney's Waimea Wall are good examples of this phenomenon. When a cliff face is oriented at an angle to the schist's foliation, erosion along the foliation planes creates parallel holds—horizontals if the foliation is flat or angling holds if the foliation is wavy or folded. The bountiful jug holds of the Bonsai cliff are formed this way.

The Conway granite that forms Cathedral Ledge and Whitehorse Ledge across the mountains in North Conway, however, is not foliated. Instead the rock has the classic homogeneous texture of granite, with an interlocking network of medium- to coarse-grained crystals. The routes at Cathedral and Whitehorse follow holds that are primarily sculpted by erosion along fracture

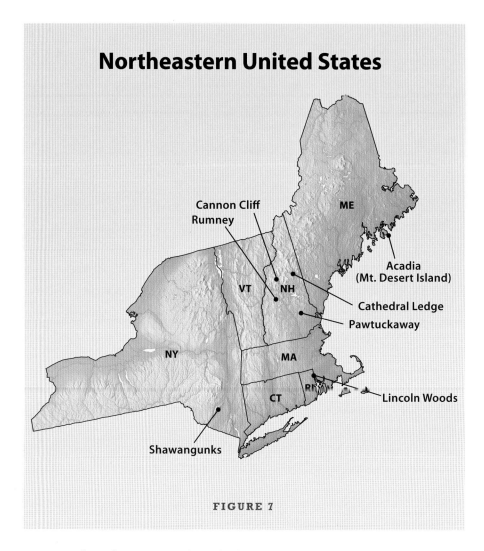

Northeastern United States

Cannon Cliff
Rumney

ME

Acadia
(Mt. Desert Island)

VT   NH

Cathedral Ledge

Pawtuckaway

NY

MA

CT   RI

Lincoln Woods

Shawangunks

FIGURE 7

systems. These fractures result in the breaking off of flakes—thin ones, to create small edge holds, or thick ones, to create off-width systems, as in the case of the Peanut Gallery Flake at Cathedral.

The presence of foliation in the Littleton schist and the lack of foliation in the Conway granite also control the types of crack climbs that are found at the crags. The foliation layers of the schist provide natural planes of weakness in the rock, so instead of cracking when forces are imposed on the rock, the schist tends to accommodate those forces by sliding along its preexisting planes. The Conway granite, on the other hand, accommodates forces by fracturing, resulting in the classic vertical crack routes of North Conway.

Rumney's Rock

The schist cliffs at Rumney are part of a thick sequence of metamorphosed sedimentary rocks, mostly deepwater shales and sandstones, that were deposited over 400 million years ago in an ocean that existed between North America and a microcontinent to the east called Avalon. These sediments were metamorphosed and thrust up onto the eastern edge of North America during a collision with Avalon. This collision occurred during the Acadian Orogeny, or mountain-building event, which was one of three collisional events that formed the Appalachian Mountains. The metamorphosed sedimentary rocks are now found in a southwest-trending band that extends from western Maine into Connecticut, called the Central Maine Belt or the Merrimack Belt. This sequence of rocks also includes the schists and gneisses that make up the backbone of New Hampshire's Presidential Range, including Mount Washington. These rocks were subjected to deep enough pressures that some of them melted, producing some of the oldest-preserved granitic rocks in New Hampshire, which are preserved in outcrops near the towns of Concord and Meredith.

References: 36, 42, 43, 81

Is the granite at Cathedral and Whitehorse Ledges the same as the granite at Cannon Mountain?

The granite you find at Cathedral and Whitehorse Ledges in North Conway, New Hampshire, is part of the same formation as the granite at Cannon Mountain and Owl's Head, two multipitch climbing areas on the west side of New Hampshire's White Mountains. All of these areas are part of the White Mountain Plutonic and Volcanic Series. The series is a group of ancient volcanoes that formed in the White Mountains during the early Jurassic period, about 200 to 175 million years ago. Similar sets of volcanoes of similar age are found in Quebec, Scotland, and Africa, which were all in close proximity to New England during this time period in the Pangaea supercontinent.

There are different hypotheses about why the White Mountain Plutonic and Volcanic Series formed. One idea is that the volcanoes formed as the North American continent moved over a mantle hot spot, similar to the modern-day development of Yellowstone and Hawaii. A problem with this idea, however, is that the ages of the separate volcanoes along the chain do

Alpine Rock Fields in the Presidential Range

The broad expanses of ankle-breaking sharp loose rock that you find in many alpine environments like the high Sierra of California and the Presidential Range of New Hampshire is called felsenmeer. Felsenmeer, German for "sea of rock," is produced under extreme freeze-thaw cycles. In New Hampshire, the felsenmeer likely developed toward the end of the last ice age (about 10,000 years ago) when freeze-thaw cycles occurred most days of the year.

Reference: 140

not progress in a regular fashion like one would expect for a hot-spot system (in Hawaii, for example, the volcanoes get progressively older as you move away from the hot spot). Another idea is that the volcanoes formed in a region of the Appalachian Mountains that had significantly thick crust as well as deep-seated weaknesses left over from the formation of the mountains. Motion along these weaknesses during the earliest stages of the opening of the Atlantic Ocean and the breakup of Pangaea could have brought up deep magma, forming the volcanoes.

The most abundant rock from this suite is coarse-grained granite, called Conway granite, which formed deep in the roots of the volcanoes. Conway granite is made up of two feldspars: alkali feldspar and plagioclase, as well as quartz and biotite, and has been dated between 183 and 155 million years old. There are also higher level rocks from the volcanoes preserved: the volcanic syenite of Sundown Ledge, also seen along the spine of the Moat Mountains ridgeline that lies just above Cathedral and Whitehorse.

References: 18, 44, 81, 86

Why does a small place like Acadia have so many different types of climbing?

Acadia National Park, on Maine's Mount Desert Island, features several different crags, each of which offers its own style of climbing. This climbing variability is a reflection of the diverse history of Acadia's rocks: how they formed and became emplaced together; and the history of Acadia's rocky landforms: how they developed and became exposed.

The classic alpine landscape of the Presidential Range in New Hampshire's White Mountains formed during extreme freeze-thaw cycles toward the end of the last ice age, about 10,000 years ago. PHOTO BY BRIAN POST

The three most popular crags of Acadia are the Precipice, Great Head, and Otter Cliffs, which are made up of granite, diorite, and metamorphosed volcanic rocks, respectively. The granite that forms the multipitch crack climbing at the Precipice is a pink, coarse-grained granite called Cadillac granite. Cadillac granite is about 380 million years old (Devonian period), and it intrudes the oldest rocks on the island, which are the metamorphic rocks of the Bar Harbor Formation and the Ellsworth schist. The Bar Harbor and Ellsworth rocks are metamorphosed sedimentary and volcanic rocks that originated in a shallow ocean basin more than 440 million years ago.

Overlying the Bar Harbor Formation is a group of rocks called the Cranberry Island Series. The Cranberry Island Series are rhyolites and tuffs—volcanic rocks—that were erupted and deposited during the late Silurian and early Devonian periods (about 415 to 390 million years ago), before the intrusion of the Cadillac granite. These rocks are exposed at the oceanfront crag Otter Cliffs. The Cranberry Island volcanic rocks have been tilted to an almost vertical orientation, and the steep bedding layers affect the shape and climbing features of Otter Cliffs. The individual layers, distinguished by their pink, purple, and green colors, represent different eruption events. The Cranberry Island Series volcanic rocks are not very extensive and have been greatly disrupted by faults, which is why you can't trace the rocks very far from Otter Cliffs.

The other popular oceanfront crag at Acadia is Great Head. Great Head is a steep, blocky cliff of diorite—an igneous rock that has more iron and magnesium than granite and is thus darker in color. There isn't an exact date on the diorite, but it is interpreted to be slightly older than the Cadillac granite, possibly an early igneous intrusion during the same magmatic event. The diorite at Great Head is actually a huge, broken block rather than an in-place intrusion. There is a whole region of broken-up rock in Acadia involving pieces of diorite and the metamorphic rocks of the Bar Harbor and Ellsworth units that are all surrounded by a matrix of Cadillac granite. The region is called the shatter zone, and geologists think that it formed during the intrusion of the Cadillac granite, when the roof of its magma chamber collapsed into a pool of the still-molten granite.

Acadia's rocks would be of little interest to climbers if they weren't exposed in steep cliffs. These landforms are the result of New England's glacial history and the current erosive action of the Atlantic Ocean. The rounded granite peaks on Mount Desert Island, including the Precipice, were shaped by the movement of a continental ice sheet that covered most of New England during the last ice age, about 100,000 to 10,000 years ago. The ice sheet advanced from north to south as the ice age progressed, and you can see this movement recorded in the hills. The north sides of these mountains tend to be rounded, smoothed by the scraping action of the ice sheet, whereas the south sides of the mountains are steep and jagged, their faces plucked by the downslope movement of the glacier (see figure 6). The oceanfront cliffs of Great Head and Otter Cliffs are shaped more by the action of the Atlantic Ocean than the glaciers of the last ice age. Wave action eats away at the base of these cliffs, creating overhangs and caves.

References: 23, 63, 135

Why are there so many roofs at the Gunks?

The Shawangunk Mountains, known to climbers as the Gunks, are famous for routes with horizontal cracks and wild, multitiered roofs. Where else in the world can you find a full-on roof in the middle of a 5.4 pitch? The geologic features that form these roofs are sedimentary bedding planes in the Shawangunk Formation conglomerate, the rock that makes up the steep cliff band overlooking New Paltz, New York. The Shawangunk Formation conglomerate is Silurian in age, about 420 million years old, formed from the sediment deposits of river systems that drained a group of mountains lying to the east. These were the Taconic Mountains, highlands that formed during the first pulse of Appalachian mountain building. The Taconics were thrust up along eastern North America when a chain of islands converged upon and then collided with the continent along a subduction zone (see figure 12).

The roofs at the Gunks have been formed by a combination of preferential erosion along horizontal bedding planes and undercutting of the hard conglomerate by the erosion of weaker rocks sitting just below the Gunks cliffs. The bedding planes in the conglomerate arose during the sedimentary rock's deposition stage, when changes in the pattern of sedimentation caused a subtle break in the structure of the accumulated pile. Today water infiltrates these natural planes of weakness, speeding up processes of weathering and erosion. Beneath the Shawangunk conglomerate is a thick bed of shale—a weak, friable, ultra-fine-grained sedimentary rock. Shale erodes more easily than overlying conglomerate, and its failure undercuts the cliffs, causing rock fall of large blocks along the already eroded bedding planes.

But still, how can you have a route as easy as 5.4 on such steep terrain? The secret to this question lies in the orientation of the bedding planes. After the Shawangunk conglomerate was formed—and after the Taconic Mountains were virtually eroded away to low hills—the region was tectonically compressed again, causing the sedimentary rocks to become folded into large, broad folds. These folds tilted the bedding planes of the Shawangunk conglomerate, causing them to dip off to the west rather than lie horizontally. You can see this dip in the shape of the Shawangunk Mountains themselves: Behind the cliff band of the Gunks, the mountain gently slopes downward to the west. This is the dip slope of the tilted beds. The dip of the beds is important to the climbing at the Gunks because it means that the holds that are formed along the bedding planes are tilted as well, making them in-cut.

The famous roofs of the Gunks formed by erosion along tilted bedding planes of the Shawangunk conglomerate.
PHOTO BY JIM THORNBURG

The folding and uplift of the Shawangunk conglomerate occurred during the last pulse of Appalachian mountain building, called the Alleghanian Orogeny, during the Pennsylvanian–Permian (about 300 to 250 million years ago) construction of the Pangaea supercontinent (see figures 12 and 10).

References: 14, 41

Why are there boulders at Pawtuckaway State Park in New Hampshire and Lincoln Woods State Park in Rhode Island?

Pawtuckaway and Lincoln Woods are two of New England's most popular bouldering destinations. These areas have a lot in common, including a

Gunks Quartz: A Geologic Mystery

The Shawangunk conglomerate is a hard, silica-cemented rock consisting primarily of small, rounded quartzite pebbles. The origin of these quartzite pebbles is part of an unsolved geologic mystery. The pebbles are made up of a distinctly milky type of quartz that is only found in quartz veins in igneous rocks. This quartz-vein material has not been identified in any of the surrounding or underlying rocks in the region—rocks that were involved in the construction of the Taconic Mountains during the time that the conglomerate was deposited. Most geologists think that the quartz-vein pebbles came from igneous rocks that were involved in uplifts of the Taconic Mountains far to the east of the modern Shawangunk Mountains and that these igneous rocks (and the Taconic uplifts) have since been completely eroded away.

The very rounded nature of the quartz-vein pebbles indicates that they were deposited in a high-energy environment like a fast-moving river, supporting the idea that their source region was far away. Small river-channel and trough formations are also preserved in the conglomerate, seen in the arrangement of the pebbles in some of the beds. To complicate matters, a recent study showed that 10 to 15 percent of the quartz grains in the conglomerate show evidence of a prior cement, meaning some grains were derived from an older sedimentary rock rather than an igneous rock.

The source of the milky-white quartz pebbles in the Shawangunk conglomerate may never be discovered, their existence at the Gunks just a hint of a former mountainous landscape.

References: 14, 41

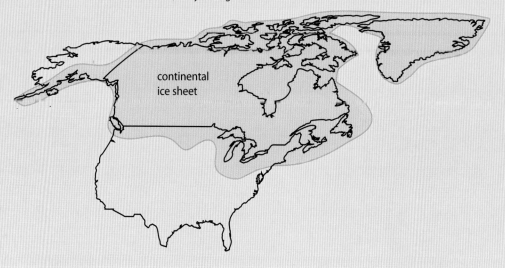

Last ice age
~20,000 years ago

continental
ice sheet

FIGURE 8
This map shows the approximate extent of the North American continental ice sheet during the last ice age (about 20,000 years ago). Alpine glaciers existed in many mountain ranges of North America during this time as well. The continental ice sheet shaped landforms across Canada, New England, and the northern states of the Midwest and West.

relatively high concentration of big boulders, a woodland setting, and nearby lakes and ponds. These are classic features of the glacial landscape in New England, formed during the last ice age, which lasted from about 100,000 to 10,000 years ago. These parks were shaped by the advancement and retreat of a continental ice sheet that covered most of Canada and the northern regions of the United States (see figure 8). As the ice sheet moved, it plucked rocks from cliffs and mountain faces it scoured over. In Pawtuckaway the ice plucked boulders from the nearby crystalline rocks of North Mountain. In Lincoln Woods the exact source of the boulders is less obvious; they could be as far-traveled as from the Canadian interior. Toward the end of the ice age, about 10,000 years ago, the ice sheet retreated northward by progressively melting at its edges. The huge boulders that were once carried by the ice sheet were dropped in place during the melting, and ponds and lakes formed from the outwash flooding of the melting glacier and its stranded icebergs.

Nicole Frati climbing a glacial erratic boulder in Pawtuckaway State Park, New Hampshire. PHOTO BY ANNE SKIDMORE

The horizontal holds on the routes in Linville Gorge are bedding planes of a Cambrian (540–490 million years old) sandstone that has since become metamorphosed into a hard quartzite.

PHOTO BY JIM THORNBURG

Southeast

What do the New River Gorge, the Red River Gorge, Tennessee Wall, and Horse Pens 40 all have in common?

These are four of the Southeast's premier climbing destinations. The areas are widely separated—each is in a different state—and they each have their own distinctive characteristics. But despite their differences, the New, the Red, T-Wall, and Horse Pens 40 are all made up of essentially the same rock. They are all Pennsylvanian-age (about 315 million years old) sandstones that formed from sediment that was shed off the growing Appalachian Mountains.

Their story begins in late Paleozoic time, about 350 to 250 million years ago. This was a time before the dinosaurs, when lush fern forests and amphibians ruled the Earth. It was also during this time that North America, Europe, South America, and Africa became assembled together into a supercontinent named Pangaea (see figure 10). As the continents collided with one another, suturing together the supercontinent, they forced up enormous mountain chains, including the Appalachians, the Ouachitas, the Ancestral Rockies, and the Urals. The Appalachian-Ouachita Mountains stretched from Newfoundland to Texas and reached heights that would rival the modern-day Himalayas.

When large mountain chains form, they place a load on the Earth's crust. This load is enough to depress the continent around the mountains, creating basins adjacent to the peaks. It's analogous to what happens when you sit on the edge of a plastic raft floating in water: The raft becomes down-warped around the load of your body, just as the land becomes down-

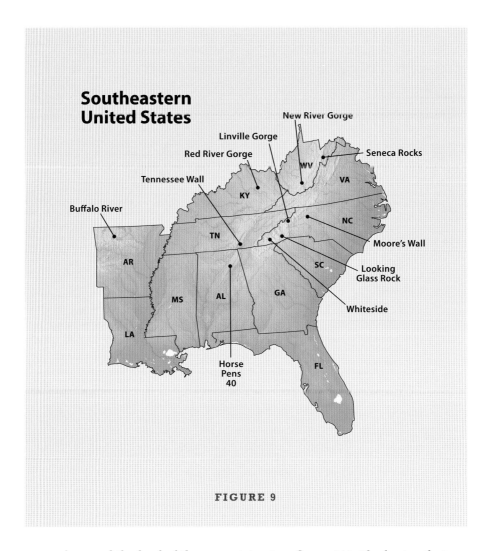

Southeastern United States

New River Gorge

Linville Gorge

Red River Gorge

Seneca Rocks

Tennessee Wall

WV

VA

KY

Buffalo River

NC

TN

Moore's Wall

AR

SC

Looking Glass Rock

MS

AL

GA

Whiteside

LA

Horse Pens 40

FL

FIGURE 9

warped around the load of the mountains (see figure 11). The basins that form along mountain chains become traps for sediment that is eroded off the rising land. Geologists study the rocks that become preserved in these basins in order to understand the history of mountaintops that were long ago eroded away.

As the Appalachian Mountains reached their maximum height, the Appalachian basin developed along the range's western slope, covering large parts of present-day Pennsylvania, Ohio, West Virginia, Kentucky, Tennessee, and Alabama. Large river systems drained the growing mountains, carrying quartz-rich sediment out into the basin in broad deltas. As the basin

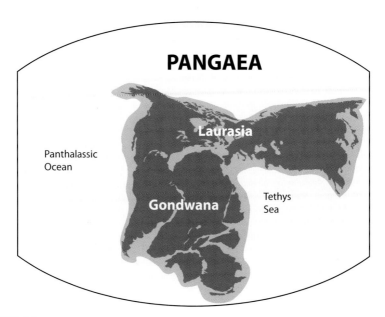

FIGURE 10

The supercontinent Pangaea included all the world's landmasses. Pangaea was constructed by several different continent-continent collisions over millions of years. The supercontinent existed between about 300 and 164 million years ago.

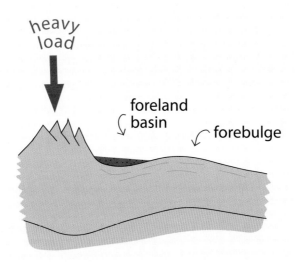

FIGURE 11

The thickened crust of mountain ranges puts a load on the tectonic plates, causing them to down-warp into basins. These basins provide space for sediment shed off the adjacent mountains to accumulate into sedimentary rocks.

filled, these sands became buried and compacted over time into quartz-rich sandstones. The Corbin sandstone of the Red River Gorge, the Nuttal sandstone of the New River Gorge, the Gizzard Group sandstone of the Tennessee Wall, and the Pottsville Formation sandstone of Horse Pens 40 all formed this way. The differences that now exist among these four distinct climbing areas were largely developed after the formation of the rock itself. The uplift and erosive history of each area and the tectonic stresses they experienced in the last 300 million years have all contributed to the individual characters of the rock we climb today.

References: 12, 27, 34, 48, 55, 60, 77, 98, 113

Is the climbing in Arkansas also related to the Red, the New, T-Wall, and Horse Pens 40?

Arkansas is littered with small crags and bouldering areas, most of which are river-cut exposures of sedimentary rock. Some of the Arkansas sandstone—the Atoka sandstone of Sam's Throne, for example—is similar to the Appalachian-basin sandstones found throughout the Southeast (the Pennsylvanian-age sandstones in places like the New and the Red). But many of the popular climbing areas in Arkansas are on older sedimentary rocks that formed before the uplift of the Appalachian and Ouachita Mountains. The crags and boulders along the Buffalo River in the Ozarks are made up of limestone, dolomite, sandstone, and chert that formed as early as 480 million years ago. These layered rocks are the result of millions of years of sediment accumulation and reef building along the ocean-covered southern edge of North America. Periodic changes in sea level are reflected in the layers: The fine sediments that form shale were deposited in the quiet waters of the deep ocean; limestone and dolomite formed in shallower seas; and the quartz-rich sandstones were deposited near the shoreline, during times of low sea level. As the sediment accumulated, the deep layers became compacted into rock. Eventually the whole package of rock became uplifted with the building of the Ouachita Mountains and the Ozark Plateau during Pennsylvanian and Permian time, about 315 to 250 million years ago. The mountains were uplifted as South America collided with the southern edge of North America during the amalgamation of the supercontinent Pangaea. The Ouachitas formed along the front of the collision zone; the Ozarks formed farther inland, in a structure called a flexural forebulge (see figure 11). The modern-day Buffalo River has since cut through the rocks of the Ozarks, carving bluffs out of the most resistant formations. The most common cliff formers are the Ordovician-age (about 465 million years old) Newton sandstone of the Everton Formation and the Mississippian-age (about 380 million years old) limestone and chert of the Boone Formation.

References: 70, 85, 142

A Short History of the Appalachian Mountains

In the lifetime of a mountain range, the Appalachians are in their twilight years. They don't compare to the young, sky-scraping peaks of the Andes or Himalayas, and their eroded slopes are modest compared with the steep pitches of the Rockies. But in the context of geologic time, the Appalachians are one of the mightiest, long-lived mountain chains in the history of the Earth. We tend to think of mountains as being built in a single event—like the collision of India and Asia that built the Himalayas, for example. But the Appalachian Mountains are the result of at least three distinct events that spanned over 250 million years of Earth history. For comparison, the Himalayas were built in less than 40 million years.

About one billion years ago, the continents of the world were arranged together in a supercontinent named Rodinia. Rodinia did not last very long—geologically speaking—and started to break up soon after it formed. North America rifted out of the supercontinent along vaguely similar boundaries to its current margins. The western boundary was along western Wyoming and eastern Utah; the eastern boundary was near the fall line of the Appalachians. An ocean similar to the modern Atlantic opened along North America's eastern edge, and the East Coast looked much as it does today, with a chain of mountains shedding sediment onto a coastal plain and shallow marine platform. In the lingo of plate tectonics, this is called a passive margin, and it lasted for over 500 million years until plate motions changed again and the ocean began to close.

The slow closing of this proto–Atlantic Ocean (called the Iapetus Ocean) caused North America to collide with at least three different landmasses over a period of about 200 million years, and it was these collisions that built the Appalachian Mountains we see today. The first collisional event, called the Taconic orogeny, took place during the Ordovician period, about 460 million years ago. During this event, a chain of volcanic islands and continental fragments

(continued)

FIGURE 12

Development of the Appalachian Mountains

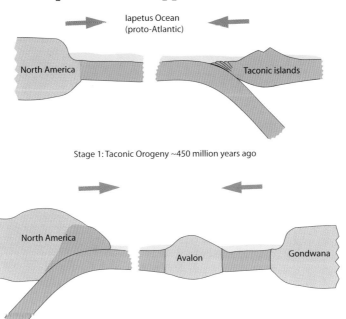

Stage 1: Taconic Orogeny ~450 million years ago

Stage 2: Acadian Orogeny ~400 million years ago

slammed into the eastern edge of North America. The details of this collision—if it took place along all North America or only in segments of the coast, if the collision involved only volcanic islands or perhaps a larger continent—are still hotly debated. But what is known is that mountains were uplifted during the collision. These were the Taconic Mountains, and they are thought to have extended from Newfoundland to Alabama. The sediments that were shed off the Taconic Mountains would later become the cliff rocks of the Gunks and Seneca Rocks.

The second Appalachian mountain-building event, called the Acadian Orogeny, took place during the Devonian period, about 410 to 360 million years ago. The Acadian Orogeny involved a collision between a microcontinent named Avalon and the eastern edge of North America, centered approximately along New England. Avalon was a fragment of land that originated off the coast of Gondwana—a supercontinent consisting of Africa, Australia, Antarctica, and India that would later collide into North America during the final Appalachian event.

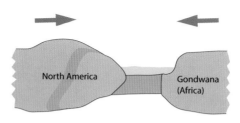

Stage 3: Alleghanian Orogeny ~300 million years ago

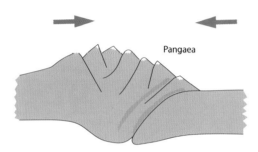

Stage 4: The formation of Pangaea ~270 million years ago

The Acadian Orogeny closed an ocean basin that existed between New England and Avalon. This basin contained sedimentary rocks that became folded and metamorphosed as the basin collapsed. These rocks now reside in a belt of schists, quartzites, and gneisses from Connecticut through Maine, making up the Presidential Range in the White Mountains. The Acadian Orogeny was also a magmatic event, creating Devonian-aged granitic rocks in New England and the Southeast.

There was a brief period of quiet before the rest of western Africa and South America, together in Gondwana, finally plowed into North America. This final phase of mountain building is known as the Alleghanian Orogeny and lasted between about 325 and 265 million years ago. The Alleghanian Orogeny brought together the Pangaea supercontinent and pushed up mountains in North America, Europe, Africa, and South America.

References: 32, 43, 46, 54, 127

Why is the Red River Gorge so steep?

Every season, climbers flock to Kentucky to get strong on the Red's famously steep walls. Carved by the Red River, a tributary of the Kentucky River, the Red River Gorge is made up of Corbin sandstone, a Pennsylvanian-age (about 315 million years old) member of the Lee Formation. But river erosion of the gorge was not the only process that formed the tilt of the Red's sandstone overhangs. Vertical cracking, weak underlying rock layers, and the erosive action of groundwater all played important roles in the creation of the steep sport and trad climbs of the Red River Gorge.

The Red River Gorge is part of the Cumberland Plateau, a region of sedimentary rock that became elevated during the uplift of the adjacent Appalachian mountain chain. As the plateau rose, flat-lying sedimentary rocks became cracked along parallel, vertical planes. These vertical cracks, called joints, have imposed structural controls on the Cumberland Plateau landforms. At the Red River Gorge, the orientations of the walls, corners, and arêtes—and the existence of numerous splitter crack routes—are all the result of these joints. Another consequence of the jointing is that groundwater is more easily percolated through the permeable Corbin sandstone. But below the Corbin is a layer of impermeable shale. When the groundwater reaches the shale barrier, it flows laterally, exiting along the cliff base as fresh springs. These springs weaken the sandstone, undermining it enough that blocks of higher rock spontaneously fall, resulting in overhangs. Below the underlying shale are limestones and siltstones, which are also weaker than sandstone, adding to the undermining that occurs along the cliff base.

In addition to steep walls, the Red is famous for its unique holds, especially smooth rails and wild networks of huecos and pockets. Many of the smooth rails and edges of the Red are formed along the sandstone's horizontal bedding planes and cross-bedding planes. Bedding and cross-bedding develop during the primary deposition of a sandstone. Bedding planes occur when there is a change in the sediment source or depositional environment; cross-bedding develops by the currents of wind or water as the sedimentary particles are being deposited. The Corbin sandstone was deposited by water currents in a large river system.

The pockets and huecos found in the walls of the Red River Gorge are called cavernous weathering. When there are many pockets close together, the formation is called honeycombing, which is a type of cavernous weather-

Janet Bergman crimps down on a bedding plane of Pennsylvanian (299–318 million years old) sandstone at the Red River Gorge.
PHOTO BY ANNE SKIDMORE

ing. Although cavernous weathering is common in sandstones, it can develop in many rock types and in many climactic environments. The origins of cavernous weathering and honeycombing are still debated among geologists, and there are several processes that may act together to form these features. Salt crystallization is one of these processes. It occurs when salt crystallizes within the pore space of sandstone, weakening and dislodging surrounding sand grains, opening the space larger. This allows more salt to crystallize, and the space grows even more. The concentration of pockets along certain layers or regions of the cliffs indicates that specific properties of the rock, even along individual beds, influence the development of cavernous weathering.

References: 34, 55, 84, 109, 124

Why do the routes at Linville Gorge tend to have a lot of horizontal holds and cracks?

The rock in North Carolina's Linville Gorge is a quartzite that is part of a group of rocks known as the Chilhowee Formation. The Chilhowee Formation is an extensive rock unit throughout the southern Appalachian Mountains, covering parts of Tennessee, North Carolina, and Virginia. When a climbing area is known for its horizontal features, it is usually a good bet that the rock is sedimentary and that the features are bedding planes. The steep, sometimes polished quartzite of Linville Gorge is a metamorphic rock that was once a sedimentary rock. It was changed from a quartz-rich sandstone into hard quartzite by tectonic heating and compression. The horizontal features of the Chilhowee quartzite are the preserved bedding planes of the original sedimentary rock. In some places the bedding planes have been transposed into limbs of tight, horizontal folds. Cross-bedding is also preserved in the Chilhowee quartzite.

The Chilhowee Formation is important because it tells us about the early stages of the first opening of the proto–Atlantic Ocean. This goes back to a time over 500 million years ago, when North America was breaking out of a supercontinent named Rodinia. As Rodinia split apart, an ocean developed along the passive, eastern edge of North America, in the same position as the modern Atlantic. The Chilhowee Formation, which is Cambrian in age (about 540 to 490 million years ago), was one of the sedimentary units that formed along this passive margin as the ocean basin expanded. This early Atlantic closed during the formation of a second supercontinent, Pangaea, about 300 million years ago. The continental collisions that constructed Pangaea thrust the Chilhowee Formation sandstones into the growing Appalachian Mountains, where they became deformed and metamorphosed into quartzite.

References: 64, 105, 120, 134

North Carolina's Pilot Mountain and Moore's Wall are far from the Blue Ridge Mountains and seem to rise out of nowhere. Are they former volcanoes?

Pilot Mountain and Moore's Wall, located in the relatively flat-lying North Carolina Piedmont region, stick out of the plains almost like the eroded volca-

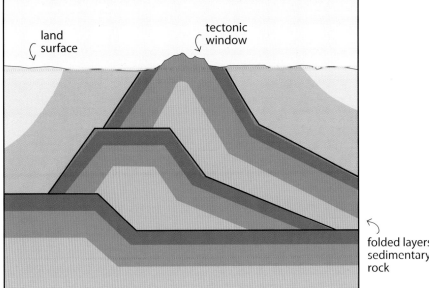

FIGURE 13
Under tectonic contraction, sedimentary layers that were originally horizontal will ramp up over each other, buckling into large folds. This folding and faulting can duplicate and thus thicken sections of sedimentary rock, allowing relatively deep layers to reach the Earth's surface. These exposures of deep rocks are called windows.

noes of the American Southwest. But Pilot Mountain and Moore's Wall aren't volcanoes or even related to volcanoes. These cliffs are made out of quartzite, a metamorphosed sandstone that is similar to the rock in Linville Gorge, almost 100 miles away. Moore's Wall and Pilot Mountain are part of a feature called the Sauratown Mountain Window. In plate tectonic terms, a window is an exposure of deep, underlying rocks. Windows form when deep rocks are locally uplifted, causing the overlying rocks to become eroded away. The Sauratown Mountain Window is a glimpse into the deep layers of the thrust sheets that make up the North Carolina Piedmont. Pilot Mountain and Moore's Wall were uplifted in a massif that formed during the stacking of thrust sheets during the formation of the Appalachian Mountains (see figure 13).

The quartzite in the Sauratown Mountain Window is about 150 feet thick, and it lies on top of gneisses and schists that are over a billion years old.

The quartzite is probably much younger than these rocks, however, and the contact between the quartzite and the other metamorphic rocks is a fault. Geologists are still unsure of the age of the quartzite: It could be the same age as the Chilhowee quartzite exposed in Linville Gorge, but it cannot be the exact formation as the Chilhowee because geologists have mapped the Chilhowee deposits thinning out to the east before the Sauratown Mountains. Still, the Sauratown quartzite could be the same age as the Chilhowee—instead of forming with the Chilhowee off the edge of North America, it could have formed off the edge of a nearby continental fragment that was later accreted to the continent during the formation of the Appalachians.

References: 22, 133

Are Whiteside and Looking Glass geologically related?

North Carolina's Whiteside Mountain and Looking Glass Rock are two of the Southeast's best multipitch climbing destinations. These are both large granite domes that are exposed in the lush Appalachian forests of western North Carolina. Despite their proximity to each other and comparable size, the granite of Whiteside and Looking Glass formed during two distinctly different times and stages in the geologic history of the southern Appalachian Mountains.

The Appalachian Mountains were built in three distinct stages, or mountain-building events—the Taconic, Acadian, and Alleghanian Orogenies. Each stage involved a collision along the eastern margin of North America, which in turn caused thickening in North America's continental crust and the formation of mountains. Whiteside and Looking Glass were formed during the first two different stages of the Appalachian Mountains: Whiteside formed 465 million years ago during the Taconic orogeny; Looking Glass formed 380 million years ago during the Acadian Orogeny.

In the Southern Appalachians, the Taconic Orogeny involved a collision between the rocks of the Piedmont terrane (coinciding with the Piedmont region of North Carolina, South Carolina, and Georgia) and the southeastern edge of North America. Geologists debate the origins of the Piedmont terrane—whether it was a group of oceanic islands like modern-day Indonesia or a small fragment of a continent like modern-day Madagascar. Whatever its origins, the Piedmont terrane likely collided with North America along a

Climber enjoying the "eyebrows" of Looking Glass Rock, North Carolina. Looking Glass Rock is a 380-million-year-old body of granite that contains numerous parallel planes of weakness, called joints, that formed as the granite became uplifted and exposed on the Earth's surface. Erosion along these joints has formed the famous "eyebrow" features.
PHOTO BY JIM THORNBURG

subduction zone. The Whiteside Mountain rock formed from magma generated during this collision. The rock of Whiteside Mountain is technically called tonalite, an igneous rock almost entirely made up of quartz and plagioclase feldspar. It differs from a true granite by its lack of potassium feldspar (see figure 4). The Whiteside rock was deformed during the later two stages of mountain building in the Appalachians, resulting in a foliation, or layering, of its minerals.

Looking Glass Rock developed 85 million years after Whiteside when another landmass crashed into North America during the Acadian Orogeny. This landmass consisted of small islands and continental fragments that were sitting offshore the approaching African and South American continents. The collision thrust thick layers of oceanic and shoreline sedimentary rocks over the edge of North America. Significant amounts of magma were generated during this collision, including the Looking Glass pluton in North Carolina and the Cadillac pluton in Maine's Acadia National Park. The magma generated during the Acadian Orogeny may have been the result of heat buildup in the thickened crust; alternatively, a subduction zone could have played a role. Looking Glass is technically a granodiorite—a type of granitic rock that has more plagioclase feldspar than alkali feldspar and also includes quartz and mica.

References: 90, 91

Why is the New River Gorge sandstone different from the sandstone in Utah?

There is sandstone and then there is sandstone. A month of pulling down on edges and rails on the steep sport routes at the New River Gorge doesn't necessarily translate to finger-stacking skills at Indian Creek. Likewise, a season of crack climbing in the desert is worlds away from the overhanging face routes in West Virginia. What is the geologic reason for the differences among sandstone climbing areas?

Even though the New River Gorge rock and many of the climbing areas in Utah are classified as sandstones, they are very different rocks. Sandstones can form in different environments and be made up of different components. This is different from igneous rocks like granites, which, as a group, are more exactly defined.

One of the most important factors determining the character of a sedimentary rock formation is its sediment source. The sources of sediment for the New River rock and the rock we climb on in Utah are very different. The New River rock was deposited by streams that were draining the Appalachian highlands, comparable to the large, meandering stream systems coming off the Himalayas today. The sandstone we climb on in Utah—the Wingate, for example—was deposited by wind in a huge desert of sand dunes, comparable to the modern-day Sahara Desert.

The New River has carved its way down through sedimentary rock formations of late and middle Pennsylvanian ages. Along the northwestern part of the New River Gorge, the river has exposed the Nuttall sandstone—a very hard and fractured sandstone of Pennsylvanian age (about 315 million years old). Original sedimentary bedding planes are preferentially eroded, providing horizontal holds and cracks.

The sandstones that are most climbed in Utah are the Wingate and Navajo Sandstones, two formations that are made up of nearly pure quartz sand particles that were deposited by wind in a huge dune field adjacent to the Ancestral Rocky Mountains. These rocks feature large cross beds and vertical cracks. They are exposed by erosion enhanced by the uplift of the Colorado Plateau rather than by a single river in a narrow gorge.

References: 48, 77, 113

Why is Seneca Rocks such a narrow fin?

The rock fin of West Virginia's Seneca Rocks is a geologically fascinating feature. The Seneca Ridge is made of once-horizontal sandstone beds that have been tilted to an almost vertical orientation. Seneca Rocks is made up of the Tuscarora Formation—a sandstone formed at the edge of an ocean basin at the beginning of the Silurian period, about 420 million years ago. The sandstones of the Tuscarora Formation are noticeably smooth and hard, partly because they were subjected to slight metamorphism at elevated temperatures and pressures. These rocks are very resistant to weathering and thus are cliff-formers wherever they crop out in the Southeast. At Seneca the beds have been tilted to nearly vertical, so the outcrop creates a steep ridge—you're essentially climbing on either sides of a bedding plane. The tilting occurred during the tectonic contraction of the Alleghanian Orogeny,

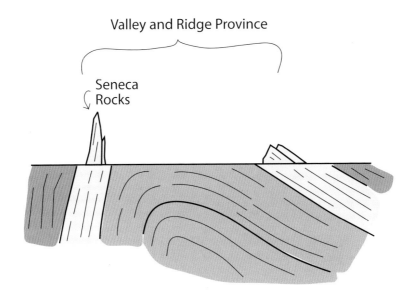

Valley and Ridge Province

Seneca
Rocks

FIGURE 14
This figure depicts the geologic structure of Seneca Rocks, West Virginia, and the Valley and Ridge Province of the Appalachian Mountain region. Resistant rock layers protrude from the Earth's surface as highlands, whereas weaker layers are eroded flat.

about 285 to 300 million years ago, which was the culminating event in the formation of the Appalachian Mountains and the construction of the supercontinent Pangaea.

One interesting fact is that the Tuscarora is the same age and is laterally equivalent to the Shawangunk Formation that makes up the Gunks. Seneca Rocks sits along the western edge of the Valley and Ridge Province of the Appalachian Mountains. This province is just what the name implies—a region of long, narrow ridges separated by elongate valleys. The valleys and ridges formed by the erosion of large folds of the sedimentary rock, including sandstones, shales, and limestones. The limestones and shales erode more easily and quickly than the hard sandstones, so the valleys form along these layers. The ridges are steep, resistant beds of sandstone. Seneca Rocks is one of these ridges. Ridges tend to be made up of the durable sandstones, including the Tuscarora Formation.

References: 14, 48, 87

Why isn't there rock climbing in Florida?

Neighboring states Georgia and Alabama have great climbing areas, so why not Florida? To make a climbing area, you need two basic ingredients: the existence of quality, climbable stone, and the exposure of that stone. Deep beneath the sand and the mud, beneath the thick layers of limestone, lies the basement of the Florida Plateau, which probably does have quality stone from the perspective of rock climbers. The problem is, there haven't been any interactions between the tectonic plates to cause uplift or mountain building in this area in over 200 million years, so it's all buried.

The basement of the Florida Plateau is made up of ancient volcanic and sedimentary rocks that originated closer to the African continent than North America. These rocks were caught in the middle of the supercontinent Pangaea over 200 million years ago. When Pangaea broke apart and North America rifted away toward its present-day position, Florida came with it. From that time on, it has sat quietly off the southern coast of the continent, building up sediments and eroding them down depending on the sea level. Most of the surface of Florida we know today is made up of limestone and marine silt and sand that were deposited across the platform during times of high sea level. The modern surface has only been exposed in the past 10,000 years, since the end of the last ice age. In the humid climate of Florida, the exposed limestones are extremely weak, soft rocks and are easily dissolved. There are very few outcrops of rock in Florida. The ones that do exist are typically platforms cut by waves or low banks along shallow river channels.

References: 1, 20, 140

Climbers on top of **Cleopatra's Needle**
at Devil's Lake, Wisconsin.
PHOTO BY GORDON MEDARIS JR.

Midwest

What kind of rock is Taylors Falls, Minnesota and Wisconsin? Why are there cliffs there?

The border-spanning cliffs of Minnesota and Wisconsin's Taylors Falls are made up of basalt—a dark, iron- and magnesium-rich volcanic rock. But the Taylors Falls basalt isn't your average Arizona- or New Mexico-type basalt: it is much older. The Taylors Falls cliffs are part of a group of basalts that formed about 1.1 billion years ago when the middle of the North American continent tried to split apart. These rocks are called the midcontinental rift system, a region much like the modern-day Rio Grande area of New Mexico, where basaltic lavas have poured out onto the continent as the crust stretched and thinned. The extensional forces along the midcontinental rift abruptly ceased, however, before a new ocean could be created and the continent could be split in two. The abrupt end of the rift system occurred when the tectonic plate motions changed and North America was involved in continental collisions to form Rodinia, one of the Earth's earliest supercontinents.

Taylors Falls is one of the few places in the Midwest where the midcontinental rift basalts are exposed. In most places, deep layers of sedimentary rock bury the basalts far below the Earth's surface. Geophysicists have been able to trace the extent of the midcontinental rift southward into Kansas because of the different properties of seismic waves moving through basalt versus sedimentary rock.

The basalt at Taylors Falls contains many vesicles, or air bubbles, that are filled with minerals that formed after the basalt, by precipitation out of groundwater. Most of the vesicles are filled by the mineral epidote, a bright

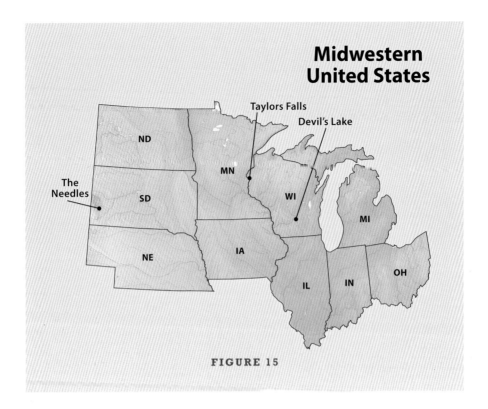

Midwestern United States

FIGURE 15

green crystal. Taylors Falls is also famous with non–rock climbers because of its enormous potholes. These circular depressions were carved by boulders caught in eddy currents during flooding of the region following the end of the last ice age, about 10,000 years ago. The intersections of joint systems (cracks) facilitated the erosion of the depressions by capturing loose blocks, which then became grindstones in flood waters.

References: 47, 137

Why are the South Dakota Needles needles?

The run-out, coarse-grained spires of the Needles area of South Dakota are carved out of a 1.7-billion-year-old granite called Harney Peak granite. The needle forms are the result of erosion along closely spaced vertical crack systems called joints. These joints could have formed during any stresses that affected the Harney Peak granite in the last 1.7 billion years. Some of the joint systems likely developed about 50 million year ago when the granite was uplifted during the rise of the Black Hills.

Liz Hajek climbing the glacially polished holds of **One Slim Fish** *(5.12) on 1.1-billion-year-old basalt at Taylors Falls, Minnesota.*

PHOTO BY JOSH HELKE

The Black Hills, including Mount Rushmore and the Needles area, up-lifted about 50 million years ago during the building of the Rocky Mountains in an event called the Laramide Orogeny. This event involved contraction and shortening along the spine of the Rocky Mountain West, forcing up deep, ancient rocks like the Harney Peak granite along steep faults.

Harney Peak granite is a coarse-grained granite that formed from the melting of continental rocks. Its age, 1.7 billion years old, corresponds with a time period when numerous landmasses started to collide with the south-western edge of North America, at that time located near the Wyoming-Colorado border. The Harney Peak granite was likely generated by intense heating of the continental rocks as the crust became thickened along this collisional boundary. Climbers are familiar with other igneous rocks of the same age, which were all related to this growth of southwestern North America. These rocks include the granitic rocks of Rocky Mountain National Park, the Black Canyon of the Gunnison, and Boulder Creek, Colorado.

References: 126, 140

Why does the Devil's Lake rock look like sandstone but feel so different?

Devil's Lake, one of the Midwest's finest climbing areas, has many features of a sedimentary sandstone—ripple marks and bedding planes—but the rock is much harder than the typical sandstones climbers find in places like Utah and Colorado. This is because the Devil's Lake rock only used to be a sand-stone. It was metamorphosed—baked and compressed—into one of the world's hardest (and slipperiest, as Devil's Lake climbers will attest) rocks: quartzite. Devil's Lake is made up of Baraboo quartzite—a metamorphosed, very pure quartz sandstone that was deposited by rivers between about 1,750 and 1,630 million years ago. This was a time when the ancient core of the North American continent first began to stabilize. The quartzite is dis-tinctively red in color due to the presence of hematite, an iron oxide mineral that is similar to rust.

Baraboo quartzite represents one of the most chemically mature sedi-mentary rocks in the world, meaning that all extraneous particles have been removed by processes of weathering and erosion and all that is left is the hardest, most resistant component: quartz sand. The formation of an ultra-mature sediment like the one preserved in Baraboo quartzite requires a peculiar environment. Geologists think that the climate of the time that the Baraboo quartzite was being deposited facilitated intense chemical weathering, likely by hot, humid conditions and high amounts of oxygen in the atmosphere. Some geologists also think that a biotic crust—mats of iron-eating bacteria like the cryptobiotic soils we see today in deserts—may have also played a role in the chemical development of these peculiar sandstones.

The metamorphism that changed the Baraboo sandstone into quartzite occurred during collisions that occurred along the southwestern margin of North America about 1.6 billion years ago. During this time, volcanic island chains and possibly even microcontinents became sutured onto North America, extending the continent edge to the southwest.

References: 47, 89

*Rolando Garibotti ropeless on
the Fountain Formation sandstone
of Eldorado Canyon, climbing
The Naked Edge (5.11+).*
PHOTO BY JIM SURETTE

Rocky Mountains

Why are most of the fourteeners in Colorado?

Colorado has fifty-three peaks over 14,000 feet—more than any other state in the United States and more than all of Canada. For comparison, Alaska, which is next on the list, has only twenty-one peaks over 14,000 feet. What is so special about Colorado?

Most people assume that the reason Colorado has so many high peaks is because the state lies in the heart of the Rocky Mountains, which are tall. By this reasoning, the uplift of the Rockies—called the Laramide Orogeny—is the event that gave Colorado its fourteeners. This thinking is on the right track and is partially true, but a key piece to the answer is still missing.

Part of that key lies with the difference between elevation and relief. Elevation is the vertical distance from sea level; relief is the vertical distance between the highest and lowest points in an area. The baseline for Colorado's fourteeners is already relatively high—the Denver basin, for example, lies at over 5,000 feet—so the relief of these fourteeners is less than that of fourteeners that begin at sea level. So now the question becomes, why are the basins in Colorado so high? Does that have to do with the formation of the Rocky Mountains?

To answer these questions, we need to know when the region went high. Was the region already high before the formation of the Rockies due to an earlier event, and the peaks of the Rockies were just elevated even higher? Or did the high elevations come at the same time as the construction of the Rockies? Or was the region raised to high elevations more recently?

Rocky Mountains

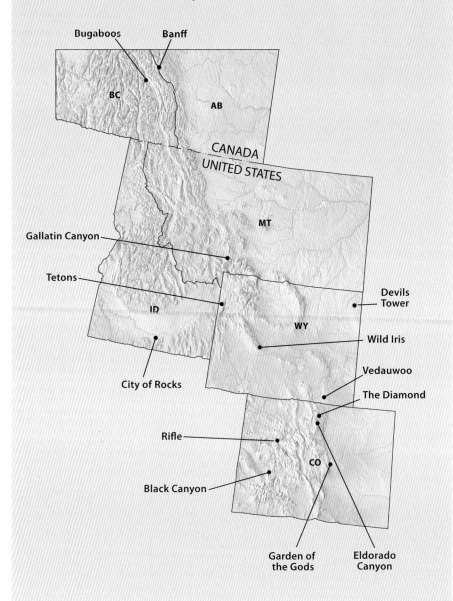

Bugaboos
Banff
BC
AB
CANADA
UNITED STATES
MT
Gallatin Canyon
Tetons
Devils Tower
ID
WY
Wild Iris
Vedauwoo
The Diamond
City of Rocks
Rifle
CO
Black Canyon
Garden of the Gods
Eldorado Canyon

FIGURE 16

Some of the high peaks in Colorado are topped with relatively young limestone, which by definition forms at or below sea level, meaning that Colorado's high elevations must have developed at the same time or after the formation of the Rocky Mountains. To complicate the problem even more, geologists have found convincing evidence that after the Rocky Mountains formed, they were almost completely buried by sediment and ash fall. The topography we enjoy as climbers today formed only when rivers began to cut down into this subdued landscape, finally exhuming the Rocky Mountains to their former grandeur. This exhumation of the buried Rocky Mountains has only occurred in approximately the last ten million years.

Based on this history, some geologists believe that the high elevations of the Colorado region are a relatively young feature, young meaning the last ten million years or so, and that the sudden downcutting by rivers and excavation of the peaks occurred because the region was vertically uplifted. The opposing view is that the Rocky Mountains reached their high elevations during the original mountain-building event, between seventy and fifty-five million years ago, and that the sudden downcutting by the rivers and excavation of the peaks occurred because of a change in climate. A wetter climate can lead to more powerful rivers, which will lead to higher rates of erosion.

Geologists often use a cutting-the-cake analogy for this debate, with the land surface represented by the cake and the high-energy rivers represented by the knife. Did the knife cut down into the cake, or did the cake rise into the knife? Did the rivers cut down into the rocks, forming the dissected landscape of the present-day Rocky Mountain region, or did the land rise up into the abrasive rivers (see figure 17)?

The story of when the Rocky Mountains reached their high elevations is far from being resolved, and there are likely more complications beyond the cake and knife story, like the possibility that different parts of the region went high at different times. One relatively recent breakthrough in this conundrum has come from geophysical work. Geophysicists have analyzed seismic waves from beneath the Rocky Mountain region and have determined that the area is underlain by anomalously hot mantle. This hot mantle is more buoyant than surrounding mantle and is probably important for sustaining the Rocky Mountain region's high elevations. The hot mantle underneath the central and southern Rocky Mountains may be part of the

FIGURE 17

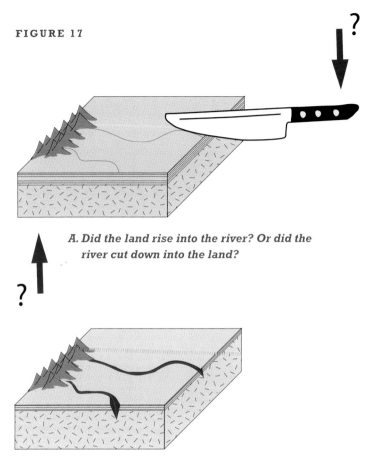

A. Did the land rise into the river? Or did the
   river cut down into the land?

B. Downcutting rivers can carve deep gorges in
   crystalline bedrock.

Rio Grande Rift, a continental rift zone that is located along the Rio Grande river valley in New Mexico. The Rio Grande Rift is a zone of extreme extension in the Earth's crust, where the tectonic plate is trying to pull itself apart. Like midocean ridges, where a plate pulls apart, hot mantle rises up to fill the created space, eventually to form new crust.

Reference: 118

A Short History of Colorado

The rocks of Colorado, magnificently exposed in the heart of the Rocky Mountains, tell the story of the evolution of the American West. The story begins two billion years ago, a time before Colorado existed, when North America's southwestern shoreline lay near the southern border of Wyoming. The Colorado Province, a geologic province that comprises much of the present-day West, including Colorado, was built along this ancient coastline by a succession of collisions with several island chains. It was as if all of the islands of Indonesia and Malaysia became swept together against the edge of the continent. Although questions still remain about the details of this assembly, the construction of the American West is one of the best-studied examples of how continents on Earth grow larger.

The Colorado Province was assembled in a relatively short period of geologic time—200 million years—from about 1.8 to 1.6 billion years ago. Following this enormous continental growth, there was an outburst of granitic magmatism, resulting in large plutons that intruded and stitched together the newly expanded crust. These plutons are the 1.4-billion-year-old granitic rocks that are exposed in Rocky Mountain National Park, the Black Canyon of the Gunnison, and Vedauwoo.

The next big event to affect Colorado was the breakup of a supercontinent named Rodinia. The exact configuration of the continents in Rodinia and the collisions that built the supercontinent are still debated by geologists. The one thing we know, however, is that the supercontinent was relatively short-lived. Rodinia broke apart about one billion years ago, and its breakup opened a new ocean basin along the west edge of North America, roughly along the western borders of modern-day Colorado and Wyoming.

As this new ocean developed, western North America evolved into a passive margin, which is a term geologists use for a continent boundary that does not correspond to a tectonic plate boundary. North America's eastern coast is a present-day example of a passive margin: The edge of the North American tectonic plate lies along the mid-Atlantic ridge, far to the east of the continental coastline. Because most geologic activity occurs along plate boundaries, passive margins are typically stable and geologically quiet.

The passive margin that developed along western North America is important to the evolution of Colorado because it allowed for the undisturbed deposition of thick sequences of sediment. Rises and falls in the sea level over millions of years

(continued on page 68)

FIGURE 18   *An Illustrated History of Colorado*

I. The Construction of Colorado: ~1.8–1.6 billion years ago

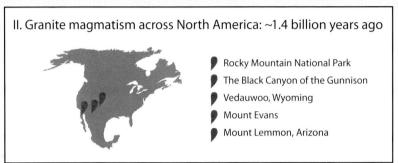

ancient North America

Tectonic collision between island chains and ancient North America

II. Granite magmatism across North America: ~1.4 billion years ago

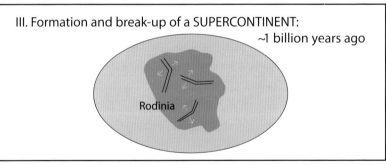

Rocky Mountain National Park

The Black Canyon of the Gunnison

Vedauwoo, Wyoming

Mount Evans

Mount Lemmon, Arizona

III. Formation and break-up of a SUPERCONTINENT: ~1 billion years ago

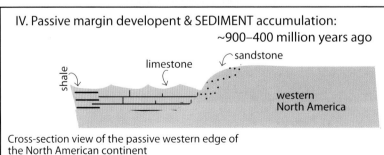

Rodinia

IV. Passive margin development & SEDIMENT accumulation: ~900–400 million years ago

shale

limestone

sandstone

western North America

Cross-section view of the passive western edge of the North American continent

V. Uplift of the Ancestral Rocky Mountains: ~300 million years ago

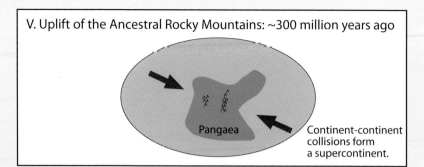

Pangaea

Continent-continent collisions form a supercontinent.

VI. Tectonic quiescence = EROSION: ~200–100 million years ago

Ancestral Rocky Mountains are completely eroded away. The sediment derived from these peaks is preserved in basin-fill sedimentary rocks like the Fountain Formation.

VII. The Laramide Orogeny: uplift of the Rocky Mountains
~70–50 million years ago

Rockies

Farallon Plate

North American Plate

Flat-slab subduction of the oceanic plate transmits stresses into the North American interior, causing mountain uplift.

VIII. Mountain burial and then uplift/excavation:
~50 million years ago to present

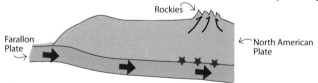

Mountains buried by volcanic ash and sediment.

Excavation of peaks due to regional uplift and/or change in climate.

resulted in the variable layers of limestone, shale, and sandstone that now dominate western Colorado and the rest of the American West.

About a million years ago, after millions of years of quiet sediment deposition, Colorado and the Rocky Mountain region became disturbed by tectonic events occurring along the eastern edge of North America. A continental collision between North America, Africa, and South America built the last stage of the Appalachian Mountains and brought together a supercontinent called Pangaea. In a relationship that is not entirely understood, Colorado felt the effects of this far-away collision, and a range of mountains were uplifted from southeast Utah through Colorado to southeast Wyoming. These were the Ancestral Rocky Mountains, and they occupied many of the same places as the modern Rocky Mountains.

The Ancestral Rocky Mountains were eventually eroded down to low hills, with their detritus collected into the sedimentary rock we now climb on in places like Eldorado Canyon and Garden of the Gods. By the Triassic period, about 235 million years ago, Pangaea began to break apart and a subduction zone developed along the formerly passive west coast of North America. Over millions of years, compressive forces generated along the subduction zone led to thrusting and folding of the thick passive-margin sediments of western North America. These structures make up the fold-and-thrust belt mountains that run from Canada to northern Arizona. Then, about seventy million years ago, something changed again in the tectonic configuration of the West, and some of the faults that once thrust up the Ancestral Rocky Mountains became reactivated, generating new mountains. This is called the Laramide Orogeny, and it is the tectonic event that built the present-day Rocky Mountains.

There are many questions that still remain about why the Laramide Orogeny occurred. Why did fracturing and mountain uplift develop deep within the interior of the continent, far from the edge of the plate, where most tectonic events take place? Most geologists think that fundamental weaknesses in the crust, possibly going back to the assembly of the Colorado Province 1.8 billion years ago, influenced the way western North America responded to tectonic stresses through time. Another idea about why the Rocky Mountains were built so far into the continent's interior is the hypothesis of flat-slab subduction. This idea is that the oceanic plate that was sliding down beneath western North America shallowed its angle, scraping along the bottom of the continent and transmitting stresses far to the interior. This is the current, most-accepted explanation for the formation of the Rocky Mountains, but the debate is far from over. Other ideas include a collision hypothesis, called the hit-and-run model. Geologists who support the hit-and-run model think that there may have been a collision between North America and a small continental fragment along the southern coast of California during the time that the Rocky Mountains were being built. They suggest that the reason we can't find that fragment today is because it collided very obliquely with California, then continued northward to British Columbia.

The story of Colorado and the Rocky Mountains does not end with their period of uplift, between 70 and 55 million years ago. Following the Laramide Orogeny was a period of intense erosion of the mountains and high rates of sediment deposition. There was a flare-up of volcanic activity to the west, spewing large amounts of ash into the atmosphere that further blanketed the region. The Rocky Mountains were essentially buried during this time, until only the very tops of the peaks were above the ground. The entire Rocky Mountain region has since been uplifted and exhumed, the basins excavated of some of their sediment, and the mountains carved into the high-angle peaks we climb today.

Reference: 117

Why is the Black Canyon of the Gunnison so challenging?

There is nowhere else on the planet like the Black Canyon of the Gunnison. The steep, massive walls; the tight, dark canyon; the infamous bands of chossy pegmatite: The unique features of the Black always seem to serve up adventures. The challenging features of the Black Canyon are the direct result of the types of rock that are exposed, as well as the history of the Gunnison River itself.

The rocks exposed in the walls of the Black Canyon are some of the oldest in western North America. They record the growth and stabilization of the Colorado Province—the southwestern region of the United States—during Precambrian time. One of the younger rocks in the canyon is the Vernal Mesa granite, a 1.4-billion-year-old rock that forms the 1,800-foot North Chasm View Wall, home to such routes as *The Hallucinogen Wall* and the *Scenic Cruise*. The Vernal Mesa rock is technically a monzogranite—a granitic rock with slightly more feldspars than quartz—(see figure 4). The Vernal Mesa granite formed during a period of widespread magmatism across North America, a period that also saw the formation of the granitic rocks at Mount Evans, Colorado; Rocky Mountain National Park; and Vedauwoo, Wyoming. The sheerness of the Chasm View Wall area is controlled by three variables: the vertical systems of cracks in the granite; the hard, competent nature of the granite and underlying rocks; and the rapid downcutting of the canyon by the Gunnison River.

Beyond the Chasm View Wall region, the Black Canyon is carved out of igneous and metamorphic rocks that are about 1.7 billion years old. Some of these rocks are highly metamorphosed versions of sedimentary rocks that once made up oceanic islands. As the Colorado Province became assembled by the sweeping collisions of these islands, the sedimentary rocks became heated and squished into hard gneisses and schists. Some of these rocks were even partially melted, turning into a rock called a migmatite.

The primary igneous member of the Black's 1.7-billion-year-old rocks is the Pitts Meadow granodiorite. The Pitts Meadow granodiorite intruded the crust during the collisional construction of the Colorado Province. Other igneous rocks to form during this time are the Harney Peak granite of the South Dakota Black Hills (the Needles) and the Boulder Creek granodiorite of Eldorado Canyon. All of these rocks reflect the intense tectonic activity occurring in western North America during the Precambrian time.

In addition to its sheer walls, the Black Canyon is famous for its pegmatite. Pegmatite is an igneous rock that is characterized by very large crystals. In the Black, the pegmatite forms extensive networks of dikes. These dikes developed during the two pulses of igneous rock formation in the region: the 1.7-billion-year-old Pitts Meadow granodiorite and the 1.4-billion-year-old Vernal Mesa granite. The different orientations of the pegmatite bands have to do with the different fracturing habits of the host rocks, which have undergone several episodes of deformation. During these deformations, small tension gashes can form in the rocks, and these are filled with hot fluids that eventually crystallize into pegmatite.

The ancient, bullet-hard rocks of the Black Canyon would never have been exposed without the downcutting action of the Gunnison River. Deep, narrow gorges are not very common in Colorado. Why would one form here? The answer has to do with something called stream superposition. The

Jeff Achey on the first ascent of the Free Nose (5.12) on the North Chasm View Wall, Black Canyon of the Gunnison.

PHOTO BY JIM SURETTE

Gunnison River was born before the exposure of the basement rocks and before the uplift of the Gunnison Region. The river started its path though the relatively soft volcanic ash deposits that came from the San Juans. As the entire Colorado Plateau and Rocky Mountain region started to uplift in the late Tertiary-Quaternary time, the Gunnison started to cut through the soft rocks, forming a canyon. Imagine a cake rising up into the blade of a knife. By the time the river had eroded through the upper stack of sedimentary rocks that you can see in parts of the Black Canyon, it was stuck; it had no choice but to start cutting through the hard basement rock. This positioning of the stream, combined with the active tectonic uplift of the region, resulted in the cutting of the Black Canyon.

References: 58, 59, 73

The rock in Eldo looks like a sandstone but climbs like a granite. Why?

Eldorado Canyon, near Boulder, Colorado, is a steep, river-cut canyon with dark red walls and routes that are known for their technical moves and precise, sometimes run-out gear placements. The rock cliffs that host these routes are made up of the Fountain Formation, which is a coarse-grained sandstone that was deposited during the Pennsylvanian and early Permian periods, about 300 to 290 million years ago. The Eldo rock is not a typical sandstone, however. Its mineralogical makeup, alteration history, and the morphology of Eldorado Canyon itself all contribute to the unique routes found at this Front Range climbing area.

The Fountain Formation is an arkosic sandstone, or an arkose, meaning that it is rich in feldspar minerals and small clasts of other rocks. Feldspars and rock fragments are easily broken down during weathering and erosion, so when these components are preserved in rocks, as in arkosic sandstones, it means the sediment source—usually mountains—must have been nearby. In fact, geologists have used maps of the distribution of Pennsylvanian-Permian arkosic sandstones in Colorado, Utah, and Wyoming to determine the location of former mountains that must have flanked the Fountain Formation basins.

Another indication that there were nearby mountains feeding the Fountain Formation is the observation that these rocks lie directly upon Precambrian granitic and metamorphic rocks—rocks that are over a billion years

The Ancestral Rocky Mountains

Like the modern Rocky Mountains, the Ancestral Rocky Mountains formed many hundreds of miles away from the active plate boundary of North America. Typically, mountain chains form as the result of contraction and shortening along the boundaries of the tectonic plates as they interact with each other. Why does the Rocky Mountain region, far from the North American Plate margin, have a long-lasting history of mountain building? Geologists have suggested several interesting ideas to explain the formation of the Ancestral Rocky Mountains, which developed near the present-day Rocky Mountains about 300 million years ago. These ideas include stresses from strike-slip movement on the west coast of North America and uplift due to a continent-continent collision on the south and east coasts of the continent.

Despite some disagreements, there is a general consensus in the geologic community that preexisting zones of weakness in the crust of the Rocky Mountain region played an important role in generating the mountain uplifts. These zones of weakness were inherited from the Precambrian assembly of western North America—the accretion of oceanic islands and possible continental fragments to the southwest margin of the continent.

During Pennsylvanian-Permian time (about 318 to 250 million years ago), the supercontinent Pangaea formed from the collision of North America with Eurasia, South America, and Africa. The forces of this collision, as well as the enigmatic tectonic forces happening on the western edge of North America, may have had just the right combination of orientation and magnitude to squeeze the Rocky Mountain region and force uplifts of crustal blocks along old planes of weakness.

older than the sandstones. In Eldorado Canyon, the Fountain Formation lies atop the 1.7-billion-year-old Boulder Creek granodiorite. This means that 1.4 billion years of Earth history are missing along the contact between these rock formations! The erosion of 1.4 billion years of sediment deposition could only have occurred if the land surface was uplifted into mountains. These mountains, recorded by the geology of the Fountain Formation, are called the Ancestral Rocky Mountains, and they occupied many of the similar areas as the modern Rocky Mountains.

The Fountain Formation is widespread along the Front Range and is the same rock formation that makes up the Garden of the Gods and the Flatirons.

The Cutler Formation, which makes up Utah's Fisher Towers, is another arkosic sandstone of the same age. If you've ever climbed in these areas, it's obvious that the Fisher Towers and the Garden of the Gods are a quite a bit different than Eldo. The Eldo rock is harder, steeper, and more reddish purple in color. The unique features of Eldorado Canyon developed during alteration of the Fountain Formation by hot water—hydrothermal fluids—that permeated the rock sometime during its history in the crust, before its exposure in the canyon walls. Hydrothermal alteration made the Fountain Formation in Eldo harder, more tightly cemented, and enriched in iron, giving the rock its distinctive color. Geologists are not positive when the rock in Eldorado Canyon was altered, but they think it could be related to heating events that occurred during the last forty million years, possibly during the period of magmatism that built the volcanoes of the San Juan Mountains.

References: 129

Was Colorado really once an ocean?

Colorado has been flooded with seawater on several occasions over the past 1.8 billion years, leading to the formation of different marine rock units, most commonly limestone. To climbers, the best-known limestone climbing in Colorado is in Rifle Mountain Park. The steep, overhanging limestone routes in Rifle are part of the Leadville limestone, a thick and extensive sheet of limestone that formed during the Mississippian epoch, about 360 to 318 million years ago. The Mississippian was a time of widespread limestone deposition across western North America; sea levels were relatively high and the western edge of the continent lay not far to the west in Utah. The Leadville limestone was uplifted above sea level during the subsequent Pennsylvanian-Permian periods (about 318 to 250 million years ago), when the Ancestral Rocky Mountains were constructed and the supercontinent Pangaea came together. Geologists know that the Leadville was above sea level during this time because the formation shows signs of karst development, which are features of dissolving limestone. They think that the Rifle Box Canyon was once a long, subterranean cavern, now uplifted and eroded into the cliffs and caves we climb today.

Prior to the time of the Leadville limestone, western Colorado experienced an earlier period of ocean submergence. This was during the late Devonian period, about 380 to 360 million years ago, when sea levels were high and ocean waters covered the western margin of North America. The

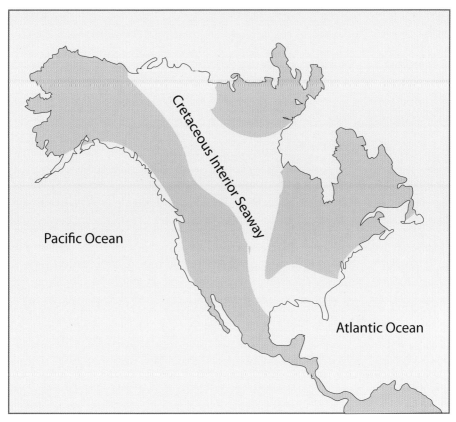

FIGURE 19
Map of the Cretaceous Interior Seaway, an inland ocean that connected the Arctic and Atlantic Oceans during a period of extremely high sea level and continental flooding during the Cretaceous period ~85–65 million years ago.

limestone cliffs around Ouray are from this Devonian marine episode.

A much later episode of ocean water in Colorado occurred in the late Cretaceous, between about 85 and 65 million years ago. During the late Cretaceous, North America looked much like it does today, with Colorado far to the interior. Rather than being flooded from the west, the ocean waters during this time were part of the Cretaceous Interior Seaway, a giant north-south trending trough that developed down the west-central part of North America, joining the Arctic Ocean to the Gulf of Mexico (see figure 19).

There are several explanations for why the interior of North America was flooded with seawater during the late Cretaceous. The climate was generally warm during this time and there were no polar ice caps, so sea levels were elevated. Some geologists have noticed that during this period, anomalously high rates of seafloor spreading and consumption of the oceans along subduction zones meant that the rocks of the seafloor were significantly young and hot, therefore more buoyant, which could have also contributed to a high sea level.

References: 25, 45

Can you find diamonds on the Diamond?

Unfortunately, there aren't any hidden pockets of diamonds to be found on the alpine rock routes of the Diamond. The Diamond is the 1,000-foot-tall east face of Longs Peak, which is one of the fourteeners in Colorado's Rocky Mountain National Park. The Diamond is named for its sheer face and angular shape rather than any presence of actual diamonds. Diamonds are very hard, crystalline forms of carbon that are only stable at extreme pressures in the Earth's mantle. They are brought to the Earth's surface along violently erupting volcanic pipes. There are no volcanic pipes on Longs Peak, however; and the rock of the Diamond's face is a granite that formed under only moderate pressures in the Earth's crust.

But the rock of Longs Peak's Diamond is no garden-variety granite. It is a very old rock called the Silver Plume granite, which crystallized about 1.4 billion years ago. There are numerous 1.4-billion-year-old granites found across North America—all the way from eastern Canada to southern California—including climbing areas like Vedauwoo, Mount Evans, and the Black Canyon of the Gunnison. Their formation is a controversial topic among geologists, and they may signify a unique time period in the history of the Earth.

Geologists call these 1.4-billion-year-old granites "anorogenic," meaning not orogenic, or unrelated to any mountain-building event. Granites are typically formed during mountain-building processes like subduction zones or collision zones, and geologists have puzzled over what tectonic conditions led to the widespread granites of this period in the Precambrian. One idea that gained popularity for a while is that the granite formed during a failed rifting event in the North American continent. This idea has fallen out of favor, however, because the chemistry of the granites does not match what you would expect in a rift zone.

One of the more creative ideas to explain these rocks is called the mantle superswell hypothesis. By this model, the enormous growth of the

The Diamond, the sheer east face of Longs Peak in Rocky Mountain National Park, Colorado, is made up of the 1.4-billion-year-old Silver Plume granite.
PHOTO BY JIM SURETTE

North American continent that occurred between 1.8 and 1.6 billion years ago served to insulate the mantle beneath it, causing a "superswell" of rising, hot rock. The superswell grilled the bottom of the continents, causing partial melting and the generation of granitic magma. The conditions of the growth of the continent and the heat in the mantle were just right during this early period of Earth history to create a superswell, something that will likely never happen again.

References: 67, 115

Why are there so many off-widths at Vedauwoo?

When you think about classic off-width climbing, one area probably comes to mind before the rest: Vedauwoo (pronounced *veed-ah-voo*). This granite climbing area is located along Interstate 80, just east of Laramie, Wyoming; and in addition to its off-widths, Vedauwoo is also famous for its coarse, abrasive crystals. (Some climbing areas just have it all.)

Vedauwoo encompasses several low hills of rounded granite massifs and boulders, nearly all of which feature off-width cracks. Vedauwoo's wide cracks developed in two primary stages: cracking and weathering. The first stage, cracking, is exactly what it seems: the fracturing of the granite by tectonic forces in the Earth's crust. The granite at Vedauwoo was likely fractured during more than one event, resulting in the segmentation of the granite body along regularly distributed and oriented systems of cracks.

The second stage in off-width formation, weathering, took place mostly beneath the Earth's surface before the granite was exposed. While at shallow depths in the Earth's crust, groundwater penetrated the crack systems of the granite, accelerating chemical weathering of the rock. Groundwater and moist soils essentially ate away at the rock, widening the preexisting cracks and rounding off their edges and corners. These weathering processes, combined with the orientation of the joint systems, created the bombay chimneys and flared off-widths that make Vedauwoo so unique (see figure 20). The two-stage development of Vedauwoo's landscape and rock features is common to many granite areas, including Joshua Tree and the City of Rocks, and is the reason traveling climbers may notice similarities among these places. Some of the differences among these areas have to do with differences in the spacing and orientation of their crack systems, as well as the weathering conditions and ages of their rocks.

FIGURE 20

The Development of Granite Climbing Areas

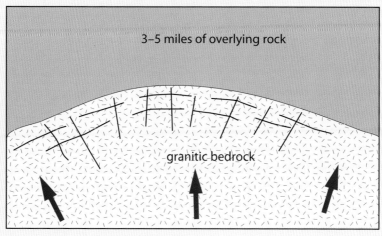

Stage 1: Cracking during rock uplift

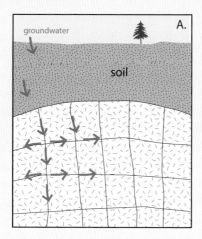

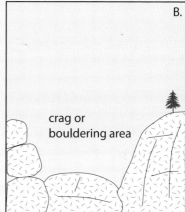

Stage 2: Weathering and erosion

There are three principal orientations of fractures in the granite at Vedauwoo—two in the vertical plane and one that is roughly horizontal—and each is roughly perpendicular to the others (see figure 20). These fractures are called joints, and they are responsible for the blocky character of many granite terranes. The development of orthogonal joint systems occurs after a body of granite cools and crystallizes from magma. The two vertical joint

Emilie Lee fights a wide crack in the 1.4-billion-year-old Sherman granite of Vedauwoo, Wyoming.   Photo by Jim Surette

systems likely develop during tectonic forces in the crust, and they can often be related to a large-scale tectonic structure, like a fault, that is nearby in the same region. The third, flat-lying fracture system is believed to develop during the uplift or exhumation of granite bodies from deep in the Earth's crust to at or near the surface. When this occurs, the granite experiences a dramatic release of pressure and thus expands in the direction of that unloading—parallel to the surface of the Earth. The expansion is accommodated by the development of cracks called sheet fractures or exfoliation planes.

The granite at Vedauwoo is part of the Sherman Batholith, an enormous body of granitic rock that is exposed throughout the Laramie Mountains of southeast Wyoming and down into the northern Front Range of Colorado.

The Sherman Batholith is exposed in the cores of Laramide uplifts, which are the highlands that make up most of the central Rocky Mountains, formed during a period of faulting and contraction in the crust that occurred between about 70 and 50 million years ago (see A Short History of Colorado). The batholith itself is 1.43 billion years old. This is the same age as some of the granite you see in Rocky Mountain National Park (including the Diamond), as well as some of the rocks in the Black Canyon of the Gunnison.

The extremely coarse nature of most of the granite at Vedauwoo has to do with how long it took for the granite to cool in its magma chamber. The more time crystals have to grow, the larger they will become. Magma can take a long time to cool if the magma chamber is sufficiently large and/ or if the surrounding rocks are also somewhat hot. The fluid content of the magma can also affect its cooling time. There are other units in the Sherman Batholith, however, like the Lincoln granite that crops out near the Lincoln monument, just west of Vedauwoo proper, that are finer grained and must have cooled quicker than the main body.

References: 53, 126

How did the formations at City of Rocks develop?

Southern Idaho's City of Rocks is a climber's playground of granite pillars and boulders, some with intricate, hollowed-out cavities and huecos. The rock at the City of Rocks is a 29-million-year-old granite from the Alamo pluton (a pluton is a body of intrusive igneous rock). During the late Tertiary period, between about 50 and 25 million years ago, western North America experienced an episode of intense magmatism and crustal extension. The Alamo pluton is just one of many granitic bodies across the American West that solidified from magma generated during this time. The granite crystallized deep in the crust, and the extensional forces at work during this time eventually uplifted the rocks to the Earth's surface. The mountains are a metamorphic core complex, just like the Catalina-Rincon Mountains, host to Mount Lemmon, in southern Arizona. (See Chapter Seven, "How did all of the different rocks of Mount Lemmon form?")

The land formations in the granite at the City of Rocks are the result of crack systems in the rock, called joints, combined with processes of weathering and erosion. Like many granite terrains, perpendicular sets of joints—formed during tectonic stresses and the unloading of pressure as the solidified granite becomes uplifted to the Earth's surface—sculpted the Alamo granite into steep-walled pillars and domes. Some of the cavities at the City of Rocks formed by weathering beneath an outer crust, or patina, on the rock's surface. Some areas of granite, while exposed on the surface of the Earth, develop a hard outer shell that contains concentrated iron oxides. If the shell becomes cracked—due to freeze-thaw cycles, for example—water and wind are able to reach the more easily eroded interior rock, eventually wearing it away until only the hard shell remains.

Some of the Alamo granite contains inclusions of other rocks. These inclusions are mostly quartzite and schists that are pieces of the surrounding Archean (two billion years old) rocks that were pulled into the magma as the Alamo granite was emplaced.

References: 7, 82, 92, 122, 126

Why does Devils Tower have so many stemming routes?

Devils Tower is a forty-million-year-old volcanic neck in the Black Hills of northeast Wyoming. Devils Tower is probably best known for its gigantic columns that create outrageous stemming routes and splitter-crack climbs. These columns are a spectacular example of columnar jointing, a phenomenon seen in many volcanic and volcaniclastic rocks, including basalt, rhyolite, and tuff. Columnar jointing forms when a volcanic rock cools, shrinking inward at a relatively uniform rate.

Devils Tower, with its dark colors and relatively fine mineral grains, looks like a basalt. But it's actually a strange rock called a phonolite. A phonolite is chemically halfway between a rhyolite and a basalt, a composition geologists call "intermediate" because it is not as rich in iron and magnesium as a basalt but not as rich in silica as a rhyolite. The strange chemistry of Devils Tower is an indication that its magma had to pass through relatively thick continental crust on its way to forming a volcano, allowing an originally basaltic magma to assimilate some silicic components of the crust. The phonolite at Devils Tower has a porphyritic texture, meaning there are large crystals floating in a fine-grained groundmass. The large crystals are anorthoclase (a form of feldspar), pyroxene, and titanite. The phonolite also has numerous vesicles, which are former air bubbles that are rounded or oval in shape and sometimes filled with secondary deposits of white calcite.

The Black Hills area was uplifted with the rest of the Rocky Mountains during the Laramide Orogeny between about 70 and 55 million years ago. The volcano that formed Devils Tower, however, was built after the uplift of the Black Hills, about forty million years ago. This volcanism was part of a time period, toward the end and after the uplift of the Rockies, in which many volcanic and magmatic rocks formed across western North America. Although the exact reasons for this relatively sudden burst of magmatism are still debated within the geologic community, most scientists think that the disintegration or removal of a subducting oceanic plate beneath North America allowed the underbelly of the continent to be exposed to hot mantle, resulting in widespread magmatism.

Geologists think that the volcano that surrounded the volcanic neck of Devils Tower probably vented to the surface through several hundred feet of sediment. Recent uplift of the entire Rocky Mountain region is responsible for the excavation of the plumbing of this forty-million-year-old volcano.

Reference: 10

What is the riddle of the Tetons?

The Tetons are one of the youngest mountain ranges on Earth, and they're also one of the oldest. Though it sounds like a riddle, it's actually just the difference between landforms and the rocks themselves—the mountain topography and the rocks of which the mountains are constructed. The rock you scale and scramble over on your way up the Grand Teton is called Mount Owen quartz monzonite, a 2.5-billion-year-old granitic rock from the Archean, one of the earliest periods of Earth history. Other peaks in the Teton Range are even older: Mount Moran is made up of gneisses that are over 2.7 billion years old. The Teton Range itself, however, is a very young feature. These incredibly old rocks were uplifted into mountains less than two million years ago, along a fault that runs across the steep eastern front of the range. In fact, the Tetons are still rising today—or rather, Jackson Hole is still sinking, making it seem like the mountains are rising. The Teton Range and Jackson Hole are separated by the Teton Fault. This is a normal fault, meaning that its topside, the Jackson Hole side, is dropped downward relative to its underside, the Tetons (see figure 21). Geologists estimate vertical movement along the fault has been as much as 7 miles.

The Teton Range is important because it tells us about the modern tectonic forces that are shaping North America today. At the same time, it tells

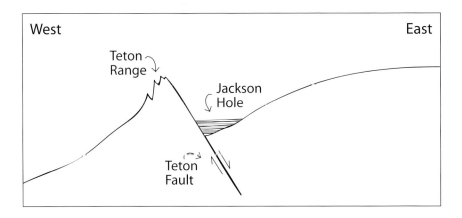

FIGURE 21
The Teton Fault is a normal fault that has uplifted the Teton Range and downdropped Jackson Hole.

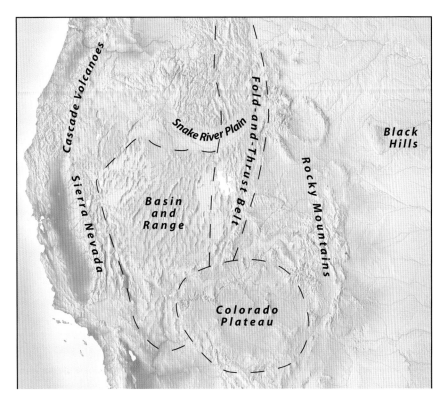

FIGURE 22
Geological provinces of the American West.

us about some of the earliest tectonic activity recorded on Earth. Normal faults like the Teton Fault develop when the Earth's crust is under extension, when it is being stretched apart. There are several active normal faults across western North America, but most of them are located west of the Rocky Mountains in the Basin and Range Province (see figure 22).

The eastern edge of this province of crustal extension is along the Wasatch Fault, which has uplifted the Wasatch Range in Utah, and the Teton Fault. The Teton Fault is also very close to Yellowstone, where there is an active hot spot, or plume of magma underneath the crust. How much the modern movement along the Teton Fault has to do with crustal extension related to the Basin and Range, or how much it has to do with the Yellowstone hot spot is still a subject of debate.

For the ancient history of the Earth, the rocks of the Teton Range, from Mount Moran north, record one of the earliest mountain-building events to affect our planet. Here geologists find rocks that were metamorphosed at depths of more than 20 miles. These are thrust upon gneisses that lack a high-pressure history, which is the same relationship we see in the modern-day Himalayas, with Tibet being thrust over India. Geologists have been able to date the ancient thrusting in the Teton rocks and have concluded that a Himalayan-scale mountain-building event occurred here 2.685 billion years ago.

A current question in modern geology is when plate tectonics started in the history of the Earth. How quickly did the Earth become stratified into mechanical and compositional layers? When did the outer layer, the lithosphere, break up into individual plates? When did subduction zones and midoceanic ridges become active for the first time? The way geologists tackle these questions is by analyzing the very oldest rocks. In the Teton Range, geologists think they have found evidence for mountain-building processes and compressional forces in a subduction zone environment. If so, that means plate tectonics were active at least 2.685 billion years ago.

References: 51, 80

Wild Iris is great . . . but why is it so short?

Wild Iris is a sport climbing area near Lander, Wyoming, that is made up of Ordovician-age (480–440 million years old) Bighorn Dolomite. The cliff at Wild Iris was uplifted with the Wind River Range during the Laramide Orogeny, the primary mountain-building event that constructed the Rocky Mountains. The height of the Wild Iris cliff—typically less than 100 feet—is controlled by the thickness of the dolomite rock layers, called strata. In general, the thickness of sedimentary strata has to do with two factors: the amount of sediment available to become deposited and the amount of space available to hold that sediment. In the case of Wild Iris, the controlling factor was space.

The Bighorn Dolomite formed out of lime muds that were deposited along the continental shelf of North America, during a time when the western boundary of the continent lay near the Wyoming–Utah border. Continental shelves are the submerged edges of continents, where continental crust is covered by a relatively thin veneer of ocean water. Sediment deposited in the shallow water of continental shelves will inherently result in thinner sedimentary rock beds because of the lack of accommodation space. On the other hand, sediment deposited out in the deeper ocean, off of the continental shelf, has more room to accumulate into thicker strata. This is why the sedimentary formations of Wyoming and Colorado are generally thinner than the correlative formations in Utah and Nevada.

Dolomite is a marine carbonate rock similar to limestone. The difference between dolomite and limestone is their chemistry: Dolomite is made up of calcium magnesium carbonate, whereas limestone is simply made up of calcium carbonate.

Reference: 4

Why are there so many big walls on Baffin Island?

Baffin Island, the world's fifth-largest island, has one of the highest concentrations of big walls on the planet, many of which remain unclimbed. Baffin's location along the Arctic Circle keeps all but the most adventurous of climbers away—and this location is also an important part of the reason the big walls exist in the first place. The origins of Baffin's big walls have to do with the glacial history of the region, as well as the structure of the island's continental crust. The origins of the rocks that make up the big walls lie with some of the earliest geologic events in North America—and the beginnings of the North American continent—nearly two billion years ago.

The most important factor in shaping the walls of Baffin Island is the glacial history of the North Atlantic. Baffin Island is the birthplace of the Laurentide Ice Sheet, the continental ice sheet that covered much of North America—nearly all of Canada and the northern regions of the United

Skiers travel beneath Mount Thor on Baffin Island. Mount Thor is one of Baffin Island's many big walls, most of which are carved out of 1.8-billion-year-old granite. PHOTO BY JIM SURETTE

States—during the last ice age. The Laurentide Ice Sheet retreated northward at the end of the ice age and started to pull back from the edges of Baffin Island about 15,000 years ago. As it retreated, scraping across the island, the continental ice sheet carved deep fiords and sheer cliffs of rock. The work of smaller, modern glaciers and the dramatic freeze-thaw cycles of the arctic are still sculpting the stark landscape of Baffin Island today.

The formation of Baffin Island's big walls cannot be completely explained by the retreat of the continental ice sheet, however—otherwise you might expect the same landscape development across all of Quebec and New England, areas that experienced a similar glacial history. The underlying structure of Baffin Island was also key to the genesis of the steep fiord topography. The structure of Baffin Island is a giant, west-tilted plane. Tectonic tilting has uplifted the eastern regions of the island, facilitating dissection and down cutting by glaciers and rivers. The uplift of the eastern margin of Baffin occurred during the opening of Baffin Bay and the rifting away of Greenland that occurred in the early Tertiary, around 60 million years ago.

The rocks that make up the Baffin Island big walls are mostly gneisses and granites that are some of the oldest rocks on Earth. Baffin Island is divided into two main geological provinces: a northern section that is part of the ancient core of the Canadian Shield (greater than 3 billion years old) and a southern section that is a collisional zone that developed during the growth of the Canadian Shield into the North American continent (about 2 billion years ago). At about 1.8 billion years ago, after the suturing together of these two provinces, an enormous body of granitic rock was emplaced into the Baffin Island crust. This was the Cumberland Batholith, and it makes up most of the peaks of the central and southern regions of Baffin, including Mount Thor and Mount Asgard in Auyuittuq National Park. The Cumberland Batholith is primarily granite and tonalite, formed from the melting of the overly thickened crustal rocks of the collision zone. The northern region of Baffin Island is older, with granitic rocks and gneisses as old as 2.8 billion years. The walls of Sam Ford Fjord are within this zone.

Reference: 72

Why is some of the rock around Banff so chossy?

The mountains around Canmore and Banff National Park are one of the world's best examples of a fold-and-thrust belt. A fold-and-thrust belt is a chain of mountains that forms when thick piles of sedimentary rock are tectonically compressed, causing sheets of rock to crumple and slide past each other, creating shortening and thickening in the crust (see figure 13). The fold-and-thrust belt in western North America affected most of the Canadian Cordillera, as well as sections of Montana, Idaho, Utah, and western Wyoming.

The North American fold-and-thrust belt formed about 120 to 80 million years ago. This was the same time as the development of a huge arc of volcanoes that stretched from Alaska to Mexico, forming the British Columbia coastal belt and the Sierra Nevada range in California. As the North American Plate moved westward over the oceanic plate, contraction between the two plates crumpled the sedimentary cover rocks, causing the construction of the fold-and-thrust belt mountains.

Most of the rocks that have been uplifted by the fold-and-thrust belt in the Canadian Rockies are layers of shale, limestone, dolomite, and quartzite (formerly sandstone) that were deposited from the Precambrian to the Jurassic along the previously quiet margin of western North America. The friable nature of these sedimentary rocks, their variable orientations from folding, and the destructive action of freeze-thaw cycles in the alpine environment all contribute to the loose rock climbers encounter around Banff.

References: 111, 130

Are the granite spires of the Bugaboos related to the granite in the Sierra Nevada?

The Bugaboos are North America's alpine granite heaven. The alpine rock spires have been shaped by glaciers and freeze-thaw cycles, enhanced by vertical sets of joints (fractures) throughout the granite. The rock itself is called the Bugaboo Batholith—a large intrusion of granitic rock that formed during the Cretaceous period, between 115 and 90 million years ago, which is the same age as the granitic rocks of the Sierra Nevada. The Bugaboo Batholith is primarily medium-grained granite and monzonite (see figure 4), and it contains varying amounts of biotite (black mica). The Bugaboo Batholith is part of a belt of granitic rocks that stretches from the Yukon to southern Idaho, and includes the Idaho Batholith and the rocks of the Sawtooths (see figure 23). This belt is similar in age, but geographically distinct from the belt of granitic rocks that includes the Sierra Nevada and parts of coastal British Columbia.

Doug Byerly approaches South Howser Tower in the Bugaboo Provincial Park of the Purcell Mountains. The Bugaboos are made up of the Bugaboo Batholith, a large intrusion of granite that is between 90 and 115 million years old.

PHOTO BY JIM SURETTE

The origins of these two belts of magmatic rocks are controversial. The western belt, including the Sierra Nevada and coastal British Columbia rocks, formed from magma generated above an oceanic plate that was subducting beneath the western coast of North America. But why would a second magmatic belt develop to the east in the Canadian Rockies?

Some geologists think that this eastern belt, called the Omineca Belt, is also related to the subduction of an oceanic plate off the western coast of North America. Because the location of the belt is farther inland, the magma had to pass through more continental crust; thus its chemistry is different from the coastal granitic rocks. The Omineca Belt rocks are typically granites and monzonites rather than the granodiorites of the coastal belt (see figure 4).

Another theory has to do with crustal thickening in the Canadian Rockies during the development of the fold-and-thrust belt. (See "Why is some of the rock around Banff so chossy?") This thickening, combined with the active tectonic setting to the west, could have caused partial melting within the deep crust, generating the Omineca Belt granitic rocks. This is a similar idea to hypotheses regarding the formation of the granitic rocks in the Karakoram, as well as some of the granitic rocks in the southern Appalachians.

Reference: 39

FIGURE 23
Geologic Provinces of Western Canada

Ship Rock, in northwest New Mexico, is the eroded neck of a volcano.
PHOTO BY BRIAN POST

7

Southwest

What is Ship Rock, and how the heck did it get there?

Ship Rock, just south of Farmington, New Mexico, is the eroded core of a volcano, often referred to as a volcanic neck. The 1,400-foot Ship Rock was exposed by erosion during the uplift of the Colorado Plateau. Ship Rock is part of the Navajo volcanic field, a group of about 80 volcanoes distributed across the Colorado Plateau that formed between 30 and 20 million years ago. These volcanoes roughly follow linear patterns on the Earth's surface that geologists interpret as the planes of former faults.

The Ship Rock volcano was an extremely violent, explosive type of volcano that forms when rising lava encounters groundwater. The groundwater, still deep beneath the Earth's surface, is heated into steam, causing an explosive eruption that fractures the surrounding rock and sends rock fragments high into the atmosphere. The volcano itself does not build above the surface of the ground the way we normally think of volcanoes. After eruption, a shallow crater, called a maar, collapses where the rock fragments were expelled, and the pyroclastic debris falls around the maar. At Ship Rock, the upper 1,000 meters or so of the maar crater and pyroclastic debris were eroded away when the Colorado Plateau became uplifted. The result is that we see the actual piping of the volcanic explosion. Most of the rock of Ship Rock is tuff-breccia, a mixture of rock fragments and ash that fell back into the pipe after the explosion. There is also some solidified magma in the tower. This solidified magma is called a lamprophyre, a somewhat rare, very potassium-rich igneous rock.

Reference: 33

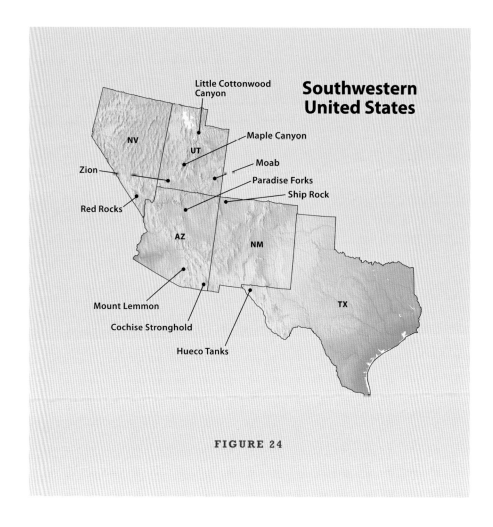

FIGURE 24

How did all the different rocks of Mount Lemmon form?

Mount Lemmon (9,157 feet), just outside Tucson, Arizona, is part of the Santa Catalina Mountains—a spectacular region for all kinds of rock enthusiasts. Climbers gravitate toward the core of the range, where the best granite is exposed. One of the most amazing features of the Santa Catalina Mountains is the close association of three different generations of granite. The oldest is the Oracle granite, which is about 1.4 billion years old and is among the oldest rocks in the American Southwest. Fast-forward 1,350 million years or so, to about 50 million years ago, and the Wilderness granite was formed, intruding into the Oracle rock. Finally, 26 million years ago, a

STRETCHING

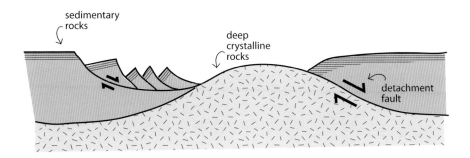

sedimentary rocks

deep crystalline rocks

detachment fault

FIGURE 25
Metamorphic core complexes form in regions of extreme stretching and thinning of the Earth's crust.

third granite intruded into the Oracle and Wilderness units, called the Catalina monzogranite.

These three generations of granite formed during different geologic settings in the development of the American Southwest, and thus each of these granites has its own unique characteristics. The 1.4-billion-year-old Oracle granite, for example, is part of a number of different igneous intrusions that formed across North America at the same time. These rocks include the granite at Vedauwoo, Wyoming, and the Diamond in Rocky Mountain National Park, Colorado. In the Santa Catalina Mountains, the Oracle granite has been substantially stretched and heated, so much so that in most places it has become a banded gneiss. The starkly banded gneiss in Sabino Canyon is made up of interlayered and highly deformed Oracle and Wilderness granites. The deformed Oracle granite makes up the distinctive dark bands in the gneiss. This dark coloring developed because the Oracle granite inherently has more dark minerals than the Wilderness granite, and also because during deformation the individual crystals of the granite reformed into flattened, ultratiny grains, which are darker than the coarser grains of an undeformed granite.

Most of the climbing in the Mount Lemmon area is on the Wilderness granite, which, especially along the southwest region of the mountains, is also extremely deformed into gneiss. If you look closely, the Wilderness granite contains tiny red crystals of garnet, an indication that it crystallized relatively deep in the crust and that it may have developed from partial melting of sedimentary rocks. Toward the core of the range, near the summit of Mount Lemmon, the Wilderness granite is less deformed and provides the best climbing.

The youngest granite in the Mount Lemmon region is the Catalina monzogranite, which forms the steep, blocky routes in the Reef of Rocks area. A monzogranite is a granite that has more feldspar components than quartz (see figure 4).

The Santa Catalina Mountains are part of a geologic structure called a metamorphic core complex. A metamorphic core complex is an exposure of deep metamorphic and igneous rocks that have been uplifted along low-angle faults during extreme thinning of the Earth's crust. The specific mechanisms of how metamorphic core complexes form are still debated within the geologic community. One of the leading models for their formation is depicted in figure 25.

A group of metamorphic core complexes developed across Arizona, Utah, Nevada, California, and Idaho all at about the same time, between about 45 and 25 million years ago. This was right after the Rocky Mountains were built, during a period of increased magmatic activity in the West. Why would extreme extension and thinning of the crust follow the extreme contraction and thickening of the crust that occurred during the building of the Rockies? This question is still an active topic of research. Most geologists, however, think that something must have been happening beneath the crust, in the mantle, to change the tectonic environment.

During the building of the Rocky Mountains, the oceanic plate that was subducting beneath western North America (called the Farallon Plate) had a very shallow dip so that, in a sense, it scraped beneath North America for hundreds of miles, creating the Rocky Mountains far inland from the plate boundary. One explanation for the formation of the metamorphic core complexes is that the angle of the Farallon Plate subduction started to steepen, allowing hot mantle to reach portions of the North American Plate that were previously insulated by the Farallon Plate. This hot mantle heated the North

American crust, resulting in increased magmatism, and at the same time weakened crust, causing it to extend or collapse under its own weight.

References: 16, 74, 99

Why are the cracks at Paradise Forks so symmetrical?

Paradise Forks, a crag just outside Flagstaff, Arizona, is in the top of the list of the youngest climbing areas on the planet. Made up of basalt cliffs, Paradise Forks is part of a broad field of young erupted lava that caps the plateaus near Flagstaff. These lavas are part of the San Francisco volcanic field, which has been periodically active in the past five million years, with some activity as recent as 900 to 750 years ago.

The coolest features of Paradise Forks are its cracks. These are called joints, and they separate individual columns of basalt, many of which are remarkably symmetrical. This morphology is called columnar jointing, and it is common in thick lava flows. The columns form as the lava shrinks when it cools. The joints between the columns are more easily weathered than the rest of the rock, so they are opened over time into perfect, vertical splitters.

The San Francisco volcanic field is part of a regional pattern of young, basaltic volcanism in the American Southwest that includes areas like El Malpais, Mount Taylor, and the Taos Plateau volcanic fields in northern New Mexico. This volcanism, still active today, is a result of tectonic extension and crustal thinning that is happening all across the desert Southwest. A continental rift basin, the Rio Grande Rift, has formed throughout New Mexico. The North American crust is also extending across Nevada, Utah, and Arizona, in a region called the Basin and Range Province.

The reasons this extensional tectonic environment developed have to do with changes in the western North American plate boundary that took place during the last 50 million years. Extensional forces developed immediately after the Rocky Mountains were uplifted, about 50 million years ago. During this time, the oceanic plate that had been shallowly subducting beneath North America may have abruptly steepened or broken off, exposing the bottom of the crust to hot mantle and thus sparking magmatism. This first stage of magma generation was mostly granitic because the thickened Rocky Mountain crust was able to partially melt. Some of these granites include the rock exposed at the City of Rocks, Mount Lemmon, Cochise Stronghold, and Little Cottonwood Canyon.

Alana Sagin negotiates the famous chicken heads of Cochise Stronghold, Arizona. The chicken heads formed by a process called case hardening in the 22–28 million-year-old Cochise granite. PHOTO BY BRIAN POST

Why the granitic magmatism switched to the basaltic volcanism we see today (starting about 10 million years ago) is also still a question of debate. The change likely has to do with the continued, long-lived tectonic setting of crustal heating, weakening, and extension in western North America. The events leading to the formation of the San Andreas Fault in California may also have played a role. The San Andreas developed when the tectonic boundary between the Pacific Ocean plate and the North American plate reorganized from a convergent boundary to a transform boundary. The cause of this reorganization is believed to be the subduction of a mid-oceanic ridge (a spreading center) in the oceanic plate. The subduction of the ridge brought hot mantle and basaltic magma to the bottom of the crust and altered the sense of motion along the plate boundary.

Another trigger of basaltic volcanism is the thinned crust. As the crust in the American West has thinned by extension, upwelling basaltic magma can more easily rise to the Earth's surface without pooling in the deep crust, where it would otherwise melt surrounding rocks and become more granitic.

References: 5, 26, 108, 123

What are all those chicken heads at Cochise Stronghold?

The chicken-head holds at Cochise Stronghold are the result of a process called case hardening. Case hardening occurs when an outer layer or crust of rock becomes more resistant to weathering than the interior of the rock. This can happen two ways: by strengthening the outer shell of the rock, or by weakening the rock's interior. Case hardening develops on all different types of rock and in many different environments. It is most common, however, to see hardening of the outside in sandstones and other sedimentary rocks and softening of the inside in granites and other crystalline rocks.

Strengthening of a rock shell occurs when minerals or salts crystallize on or within the surface of a rock, being either drawn up from the interior of the rock or accumulated on the surface from external sources (windblown dust, for example, in the case of desert varnish). Weakening of the rock's interior occurs when the rock's core is attacked by chemical weathering, usually by the penetration of groundwater along small cracks.

Whichever way the case hardening developed, chicken heads can form when the harder outer shell cracks, facilitating erosion of the interior. The chicken heads are these remnant pieces of the rock's case-hardened shell.

Cochise Stronghold is made up of Stronghold granite, a coarse-grained granite that is early Miocene to Oligocene age, about 22 to 28 million years old. There are several granitic rocks of approximately this same age across the American West, including the granite at the City of Rocks in Idaho; some of the granite at Mount Lemmon, Arizona; the Little Cottonwood Canyon granite in Utah; and the syenite at Hueco Tanks, Texas. These rocks are part of a flare-up of volcanic and magmatic activity that occurred when the subducting Farallon Plate steepened or was removed beneath North America.

References: 37, 38, 119

Why can't you climb at Red Rocks after it rains, even if it's dry?

Most of the rock climbing in the Red Rock Canyon National Conservation Area, outside Las Vegas, is on cliffs of Aztec sandstone. Aztec sandstone is a Jurassic-age rock (between about 200 and 145 million years old) that is composed of windblown sand grains. Although Las Vegas lies in one of the driest spots of North America, the region which still experiences rain can ruin the climbing for days. The reason rainwater has such a big effect on the climbing in Red Rocks is that the Aztec sandstone is very porous, meaning it soaks up the moisture and becomes weakened. Red Rocks locals will tell you about holds breaking and gear ripping out of the stone if you don't wait long enough to climb after a storm.

Why is wet sandstone weaker than dry sandstone? This is a question of importance not just to rock climbers but also to builders and engineers who use sandstone in construction. There are actually several different mechanisms by which rocks are weakened by moisture. Experiments have shown that the most important mechanism is called stress corrosion. This is a process that takes place when the chemical bonds between atoms of silica and oxygen—which are typically fairly strong—react with water, forming weak hydrogen bonds. This reaction happens within the individual quartz crystals of the sandstone and is more easily accomplished on the already-stressed bonds that exist on the tips of microcracks. The development of weakened chemical bonds changes the overall competency of the rock, allowing preexisting microcracks to propagate into larger cracks resulting in rock failure.

Another mechanism by which water weakens sedimentary rocks is by altering or softening the rock's matrix. Sandstones that are cemented by clay minerals or calcite, as is the case with the Aztec sandstone, are particularly susceptible to matrix softening. Sandstones that are cemented by quartz are less susceptible to this process because silica is not easily dissolved by water.

References: 40, 65

Why is there limestone in some parts of Nevada and sandstone in others?

Nevada is famous among rock climbers for its high-quality limestone and sandstone climbing areas. The reasons you may find limestone in one part of Nevada and sandstone in another have to do with the depositional history of the state's sedimentary rocks as well as the tectonic history of the region, which allowed the rocks to become uplifted and exposed into steep crags.

Some of Nevada's best-known climbing areas, like Red Rocks, Mount Charleston, and Mount Potosi, are part of the northwest-trending ridgeline of the Spring Mountains. Mount Charleston and Mount Potosi mark the endpoints of this range, and Red Rocks lies in the middle. The Spring Mountains are part of North America's fold-and-thrust belt, a belt of mountain ridges that formed under contractional forces during Jurassic-Cretaceous times (about 200 to 65 million years ago). The fold-and-thrust belt mountains were built by the movement of large sheets of sedimentary rock that ramped up over each other, thickening the western North America crust. These thrust sheets moved along extensive, low-angle faults that brought deeper, older sedimentary rocks up on top of younger rocks, creating an inverted stratigraphy. You can see this relationship at Red Rocks, where the sandstones are actually younger than the higher, overlying limestones.

The Spring Mountains mark the eastern boundary of the fold-and-thrust belt, and the bulk of Nevada was shaped by a different tectonic history. If you look at a shaded relief map of Nevada (see figure 22), you might notice that most of the state is made up of very regularly spaced north-south trending ridges, separated by north-south trending basins. This is the topography of the Basin and Range Province, a region of western North America that developed by steep normal faulting caused by extensional forces in the crust. In fact, for most of North America's geologic history, Nevada was much narrower. It has been stretched and expanded more than 100 percent in the last 20 million years by normal faulting.

The rocks that are exposed by the fold-and-thrust belt and the Basin and Range Province include thick sequences of Paleozoic sedimentary rocks and thinner layers of Mesozoic sedimentary rocks. During the Paleozoic era (about 550 to 250 million years ago), Nevada sat along the edge of the North American continent, and for much of this time, its land surface was submerged beneath a western ocean. The millions of years that Nevada spent underwater created the abundant limestone formations in the state, including the rocks of Mount Charleston and Mount Potosi. During the Mesozoic era, however (about 250 to 70 million years ago), intermittent tectonic activity across western North America caused Nevada to spend more time above sea level, leading to the deposition of terrigenous sediments like sandstone.

References: 21, 102, 118

Why does Hueco have so many huecos?

Hueco Tanks State Historic Site near El Paso, Texas, is named for its numerous huecos—spherical pockets and small, hollowed-out basins in the bedrock. The word "hueco" is Spanish for hollow. To climbers, the huecos make fantastic hand- and footholds; these features, along with the expansive exposures of the Hueco rock and the agreeable climate of southwest Texas, make Hueco Tanks one of the world's most popular bouldering destinations.

The reasons Hueco Tanks has so many huecos have to do with the erosion history of Hueco's crystalline bedrock. Hueco's erosion history, in turn, has to do with the more extended geologic history of the rock formations and the tectonic history of western North America.

The rock at Hueco Tanks is an intrusive igneous rock called a syenite porphyry. A syenite is an igneous rock that is characterized by having very little quartz and a whole lot of potassium feldspar in its composition (see figure 4). The Hueco syenite also includes plagioclase feldspar, biotite, and pyroxene. The word "porphyry" comes from the porphyritic texture of the Hueco syenite, meaning that there are coarse-grained minerals surrounded by a fine-grained matrix of other minerals. The coarse crystals in the Hueco syenite are made up of feldspar and biotite. The feldspar crystals are very hard and more resistant to erosion than the rock's matrix, which is why in places you can find them sticking out of the rock like little white knobs.

The Hueco syenite intruded into a bedrock of Permian limestone about 34 million years ago. The intrusion did not reach the surface, but rather bowed

Heather Baer cranks on the famous pocket holds of Hueco Tanks, Texas. These "huecos" are a form of cavernous weathering, a style of weathering that can develop when salts crystallize in small spaces in a rock and in the process dislodge adjacent grains, creating pockets. PHOTO BY JIM SURETTE

up overlying limestone strata into a domelike formation called a laccolith. The uplift of the overlying limestone rocks made them susceptible to erosion, which, over time, uncovered and exposed the syenite. The exposure of the syenite porphyry has led to its weathering, resulting in the formation of its famous huecos (see next question) and, in places, a hard, iron-rich patina. This iron patina, also called iron film or iron skin, developed when iron was freed from some of the rock's minerals during chemical weathering.

References: 8, 28

Cavernous weathering in limestone, usually by dissolution, provides creative gear placements.
Photo by Jim Surette

How do huecos form?

Whether carved out of granite, sandstone, or limestone, climbers will call most spherical, hollow holds "huecos," after the rock formations at Hueco Tanks. To geologists they're more commonly called honeycombing, alveoli, tafoni, or cavernous weathering. Whatever you call them, huecos are a fascinating feature because they seem to develop on almost any type of rock and in almost any type of environment.

Early studies of cavernous weathering concluded that wind created the rounded, hollow forms. But it is now widely accepted that wind has actually less to do with the development of these features than the processes of salt crystallization and chemical weathering.

Salt crystallization occurs when salts find their way into tiny spaces in a rock, between sand grains in a sandstone, or along microscopic cracks in a crystalline rock. The salt crystals absorb water and expand, putting pressure on adjacent grains and causing some of them to become dislodged. When grains are dislodged, the space becomes larger, causing more salts to land and crystallize there than elsewhere in the rock. This creates a feedback effect, leading to faster excavation of certain areas than others, thus forming huecos. The salts that find their way into tiny spaces in the rock to begin the process of hueco formation can come from windblown dust, water running across the rock, or even moist soils.

Chemical weathering is another important process in the formation of spherical rock cavities, especially in materials that are easily dissolved, like calcium carbonate. Water pooling in fractures in limestone can create small caverns; similarly, water trapped in sandstones that are cemented by calcite can eat away the rock into rounded hollows.

References: 96, 124, 125

Why is Indian Creek so splitter?

When you think of splitter cracks, there are few places in the world as classic as Indian Creek, a crack-climbing mecca just south of Moab, Utah. The red cliff line walling in the Indian Creek basin stretches out like a ribbon in all directions. This cliff-forming rock is Wingate sandstone, a sedimentary rock made up of windblown particles of quartz sand deposited in a vast desert about 200 million years ago during the Triassic period. The Wingate cliffs can

Janet Bergman climbs Scarface (5.11-),
*one of thousands of vertical joints in
the Wingate sandstone in Indian Creek.*
PHOTO BY JIM SURETTE

be found throughout the desert Southwest and are a common landmark of the southern Utah desert. But if these cliffs are so common, why is there only one Indian Creek? Why aren't there perfect crack climbs in every outcrop of the Wingate?

The reason behind Indian Creek's high concentration of crack climbs is location. Indian Creek, at the entrance to Canyonlands Needles region, is near the crest of a broad fold in the sedimentary layers. The fold is wide and shallow enough that the sedimentary layers at Indian Creek appear to be undeformed and flat lying. But these rocks are subtly folded, and the result of that folding is the development and opening of vertical fractures.

At first it doesn't make sense—how do the compressional forces that cause rock folding also force open cracks, which we generally associate with tensional forces? The answer to this conundrum lies in the different scales of the phenomena. Large-scale contraction in the crust can cause regionally significant folds, or upwarps, out of flat layers. On a small, local scale, however, the rock layers are stressed during folding in a stretching orientation along the fold's crest (see figure 26). In the case of Indian Creek, the fold is more like a broad bulge and is called the Monument Upwarp. This uplift, along with the San Rafael Swell, occurred during the formation of the Rocky Mountains. The crest of the Monument Upwarp lies in the Needles District of Canyonlands National Park, just a few miles west of Indian Creek. Here the rocks are considerably more fractured than even at Indian Creek, so much so that they have been eroded into the towers and hoodoos of the park.

Another reason for the fracturing of the Wingate along Indian Creek is the presence of salt at depth, below the sandstone in a buried layer called the Paradox Formation. This salt dissolves in the presence of groundwater and can lead to slumping of the land, which also causes fracturing.

The Wingate sandstone is great for climbing because it is a relatively competent, hard rock formation. But have you ever noticed that where the Wingate is the uppermost layer of rock, where there is no caprock, the cliffs are soft and rounded, often not suitable for climbing? This is because the overlying Kayenta Formation—a sequence of stream-deposited sands and clays—is instrumental in protecting the underlying Wingate from erosion.

References: 6, 7

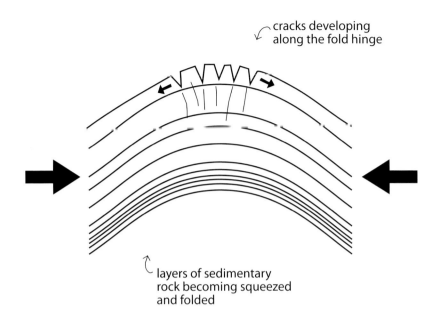

cracks developing
along the fold hinge

layers of sedimentary
rock becoming squeezed
and folded

FIGURE 26
Tension cracks can open and develop along the hinges of rock folds.

How did Castleton Tower form?

Castleton Tower, in Castle Valley, Utah, is an icon of desert climbing. The tower is carved out of a narrow fin of Wingate sandstone, which is the same rock of Indian Creek and many other climbing areas in the Moab region. The towers stand on lower angled slopes made up of shales and siltstones of the underlying Chinle and Moenkopi Formations (see figure 27). Castleton's symmetrical morphology is the result of weathering along perpendicular sets of vertical fractures, called joints. These joint systems developed during the downdropping of Castle Valley by the collapse of a salt anticline.

A salt anticline is an upwarp, or fold, of sedimentary layers created by the movement of a salt layer beneath the rock (see figure 28). In this case, the salt is part of the Paradox Formation, a sedimentary formation deep in

FIGURE 27
Common Sedimentary Rocks of the Colorado Plateau

YOUNGER	Wasatch Formation	Tertiary
	Mesaverde sandstone	
	Mancos shale	Cretaceous
	Dakota sandstone	
	Morrison Formation	
	Curtis Formation	
	Entrada sandstone	Jurassic and Triassic
	Navajo sandstone	
	Kayenta limestone	
	Wingate sandstone	
	Chinle shale	
	Moenkopi Formation	
	Cutler Formation	
	Kaibab limestone	Permian and Pennsylvanian
	White Rim sandstone	
	Paradox Formation salt	
	Molas Formation	Mississippian
	Leadville limestone	
OLDER	Ouray limestone	Devonian

FIGURE 28
How Valleys Form from the Collapse of Salt Anticlines

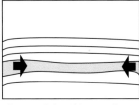

Stage 1: Salt within a stack of sedimentary layers begins to flow.

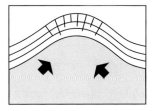

Stage 2: Flowing salt bulges the overlying rocks into an anticline (n-shaped fold).

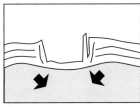

Stage 3: Groundwater dissolves the salt, causing the anticline to collapse into a valley.

Castleton Tower, in southeast Utah, formed by erosion along vertical joints in the Wingate sandstone.

the pile of sedimentary layers in this region. The Paradox Formation is exposed at the very bottom of some of the canyons along the Colorado River. The Paradox salt was deposited during the time of the Ancestral Rocky Mountains—a group of high mountains known as the Ancestral Front Range, the Wet Mountains, the Sawatch Uplifts, the San Luis Uplift, and the Uncompaghre Uplift. As the mountains were raised along faults, the land adjacent to them sagged into deep valleys. The valley southwest of the Uncompaghre Uplift was deep enough that a small, inland seaway formed called the Paradox Sea. This body of water was periodically connected to the ocean because of high global sea levels and then cut off when sea level dropped. When the Paradox Sea became completely isolated, the water evaporated, leaving thick salt deposits in the basin. Over millions of years of this process, the salt thicknesses in the Paradox basin reached thousands of feet. Sediments from the Ancestral Rocky Mountains continued to shed into the basin, eventually burying the salt.

Salt is an interesting substance. If you confine a layer of salt under high pressures, it will begin to squish around like jelly, flowing from regions of high pressure to regions of low pressure. When the salt becomes confined laterally, it will flow upward, forcing up the layers of rock above it into a gigantic fold. The forces that uplifted the Ancestral Rocky Mountains put stresses on the buried salt enough to make it flow and thicken, pushing up folds in the overlying rock. These folds are called salt-cored anticlines. When the salt reaches high enough in the Earth's surface, it encounters the water table and becomes dissolved. Then, without the support of the rising salt, the overlying rock layers collapse, forming a valley.

Many of the valleys around Moab were formed this way, including the Moab Valley itself and Castle Valley. The overlying rocks become cracked during both their upwarping and collapse, and erosion over time has exploited those cracks, forming fins and towers.

References: 7, 76, 96

What's the deal with all those cobbles in Maple Canyon?

The cobbles protruding from the sport-climbing walls of Maple Canyon, Utah, are river stones that have been compacted and cemented together into a conglomerate. Conglomerates are uncommon rocks for climbing areas because of the tendency of their large clasts to loosen and break. The Maple Canyon rock, however, is tightly welded together, making it one of the more competent conglomerate formations in western North America.

The Maple Canyon conglomerate is a member of the Price River Formation, a relatively widespread sheet of accumulated river sediments that was deposited during the late Cretaceous, about 83 to 70 million years ago. The arrangement of the cobbles in the Price River conglomerate tells geologists that the ancient river that deposited these stones was flowing toward the east. The cobbles themselves are primarily made up of quartzite and limestone. The quartzite cobbles tend to be white, pink, and red, while the limestone cobbles are commonly shades of gray and blue.

The Maple Canyon cobbles were derived from the fold-and-thrust belt mountains to the west. The fold-and-thrust belt developed during a time of compressional tectonic forces along the western boundary of North America. These forces caused shortening in the continental crust, which was accommodated by the buckling and sliding of thick sheets of sedimentary rock over each other, forming mountains. The fold-and-thrust mountains placed new loads on the crust, causing depressions called foreland basins to form adjacent to the uplifts. The rocks of the Price River Formation were deposited in one of these foreland basins.

References: 68, 138

Why are there big walls in Zion?

The red sandstone big walls of Zion National Park are relatively young geomorphic features that are growing taller even today. These walls form a broad canyon along the North Fork of the Virgin River, which is cutting its way down into the relatively soft and fractured sedimentary rocks of this part of the Colorado Plateau. The walls themselves are carved out of the Navajo sandstone, which is a thick unit of windblown quartz sands. Vertical fracture systems in the Navajo contribute to the vertical nature of Zion's walls. The fractures are also important because they facilitate the transport of rainwater down to the base of the sandstone, where it runs into an impermeable layer of shale in the underlying Kayenta Formation. Unable to flow downward, the water flows outward at fresh springs, which weakens the Navajo sandstone at its base and causes rock fall from above.

The North Fork of the Virgin River has rapidly cut down through the soft sedimentary rocks of the Colorado Plateau, forming the big walls of Zion National Park.

PHOTO BY BRIAN POST

If you only visit Zion in the dry season, you might doubt the carving abilities of such a mellow river. But during the wet season, the North Fork of the Virgin River and its surrounding tributaries are flooded, becoming powerful erosive agents. The North Fork of the Virgin River is cutting down so rapidly, in fact, that the smaller tributaries with less water flowing through them cannot keep up. This has caused the hanging valleys of Zion, like Angels Landing.

It is easy to think about a river cutting down into layers of rock, but the reverse may be true instead: that the layers of rock are rising into the river. Deeply incised gorges across the Southwest have caused geologists to wonder which scenario is taking place. Many believe that rock uplift is as important, if not more so, than river downcutting.

References: 63, 96, 124, 140

Where did the granite in Little Cottonwood Canyon come from?

The granite crags of Little Cottonwood Canyon, near Salt Lake City, Utah, are part of the Little Cottonwood stock, a relatively small pluton that ranges from granite to granodiorite in composition. The Little Cottonwood stock crystallized between 30 and 37 million years ago along with ten or so other small plutons in the western Wasatch Range.

These plutons were emplaced during a period of intense magmatism across the western United States, primarily in Nevada, Idaho, and Arizona. The reasons behind this magmatism are still debated. The Rocky Mountains had formed just prior to this time due in part to the shallow subduction of an oceanic plate along the western margin of North America. The removal of this oceanic slab from beneath the Rocky Mountain region, either by rolling back toward the oceanic trench in California or by breaking off and sinking into the deep mantle, could have brought hot mantle to the base of the continental crust, causing a pulse of magmatism. Another explanation for the magmatism is a model in which the thickened continental crust of the Rocky Mountain region was fundamentally unstable and collapsed under its own weight. It collapsed by extensional faulting and thinning, allowing hot mantle to upwell into the base of the crust and cause melting.

The Little Cottonwood stock formed about 5 miles beneath the surface of the Earth and was then uplifted along with the rest of the Wasatch

Mountains along the Wasatch Fault, starting about 15 million years ago and continuing today. The Wasatch Fault is one of the more obvious faults of the American West: It is the west-facing scarp of the Wasatch Mountains overlooking Salt Lake City. By all estimates, the Wasatch Fault is still active and has the potential to produce large-magnitude earthquakes in northern Utah.

References: 118, 132

The Wingate sandstone is a prominent cliff-former in the desert Southwest.
PHOTO BY SARAH GARLICK

The knob holds of the rock near Tuolumne Meadows are large crystals of potassium feldspar. These crystals are much larger than the surrounding minerals in the granite, and they are more resistant to weathering, which is why they stick out.
PHOTO BY JIM THORNBURG

8

California

Why is there good bouldering in Bishop? How is the bouldering related to the climbing in Owens River Gorge?

The high concentration of large, sometimes bizarrely shaped boulders near Bishop, California, make this small town in the eastern Sierra Nevada a top destination among boulderers. One of the most popular bouldering areas near Bishop is the Buttermilks, an area littered with massive granite blocks. The granite of the Buttermilks is part of the huge volume of granitic intrusions that invaded the Californian crust, forming the backbone of the Sierra Nevada between about 120 and 80 million years ago. Millions of years of weathering and erosion on the Earth's surface have shaped the Buttermilk boulders out of what was once a larger, coherent body of rock.

But if the Buttermilks granite is similar to the rest of the granite in the Sierra Nevada, why aren't there more areas like the Buttermilks all over California? The answer lies in the formation of the Owens River Valley, in which the Buttermilks lie. The Owens River Valley is a block of the Earth's crust that has been dropped down relative to the surrounding land along steep faults. Because of this downdropping, the granitic rocks of the Buttermilks were exposed to weathering and erosion conditions of lower elevations than most of the granitic rocks of the High Sierra. Instead of glaciers and melt-freeze cycles affecting the rocks, the low-lying granite was instead broken down and shaped by a process of chemical weathering.

The rock of the Happy and Sad bouldering areas is an altogether different beast than rock of the Buttermilks. The giant eggs of the Happy and Sads are riddled with pockets and small, fragmented inclusions. These

California

Yosemite

Tuolumne Meadows

Owens River Gorge and Bishop Bouldering

CA

Joshua Tree

FIGURE 29

boulders are made up of welded volcanic ash of the Bishop tuff. Compared to the ninety-million-year-old (or thereabouts) granite of the Buttermilks, the Happy and Sad boulders were practically born yesterday. The Bishop tuff is an enormous sheet of ash that fell from an erupting volcano about 730,000 years ago. The volcano that spewed all this ash is centered near the town of Mammoth, although ash fell as far away as present-day Nebraska and Kansas. Geologists estimate that the size of the Mammoth eruption was bigger than any volcanic eruption in human recorded history. The sport climbing in Owens River Gorge is also on Bishop tuff. The Owens River, a powerful erosive force before all its water was diverted to Los Angeles, cut the steep walls of the gorge through the relatively soft Bishop tuff. Climbers now use horizontal joints, flattened chunks of pumice, and air pockets as hand- and footholds on the cliffs and boulders of the tuff.

References: 116, 126

The Buttermilk boulders near Bishop, California, are blocks of Sierra Nevada granite that have been chemically weathered in the warmer climate of Owens Valley.

PHOTO BY ANNE SKIDMORE

What is the North America Wall on El Capitan?

El Capitan's granite walls rise over 2,000 feet above the valley floor in Yosemite National Park. Within El Cap's east wall there is a dark body of rock shaped like the North American continent. Route names like the *North America Wall,* the *Pacific Ocean Wall, South Seas,* and *New Jersey Turnpike* come from this startling feature. So how did it form?

The dark rock is called diorite, and it intruded the El Capitan granite as magma after the El Capitan granite had already solidified. Diorite, like granite, is an intrusive igneous rock, but it has a higher percentage of dark minerals than granite. These minerals, usually biotite or hornblende, owe their dark colors (black to dark brown and green) to the presence of iron and magnesium. There are actually two different sets of diorite intrusions on El Capitan's east face. The oldest set can be seen at the base of the wall. Here dikes and wedge-shaped pods of diorite are surrounded by a light-colored rock that has a foliation, a layering formed by the alignment of minerals. This light-colored rock is El Capitan granite that became heated and squeezed when the diorite magma pushed through.

The second set of intrusions forms two complex dike bodies: a western body that is shaped like North America and an eastern body that surrounds a circular area of white El Capitan granite—the Great Circle of the Zodiac wall. The shapes of these bodies are the result of the path that the diorite magma took as it invaded the granite, and also the interactions that occurred between the magma and granite during emplacement. Many geologists think that the diorite partially melted the surrounding granite as it intruded, forming hybrid rocks and complex shapes. The western body's resemblance to the North American continent is just a neat coincidence.

The oldest set of diorite dikes intruded the El Capitan granite early in its history, when the granite was still cooling, about 102 million years ago. The younger set of dikes is related to intrusion of the Taft granite that makes up Glacier Point Apron, which occurred about 96 million years ago.

References: 71, 104, 106

How did the formations in Joshua Tree develop?

The famously rounded and cracked rock formations of Joshua Tree National Park have been attracting climbers for over five decades. The Joshua Tree

The North America Wall lies in the central, east face of El Capitan, on the right side of this photograph. The wall is named after a set of diorite intrusions that take on the vague shape of the North American continent.

PHOTO BY JIM SURETTE

boulders and cliffs are sculpted by agents of weathering and erosion along preexisting crack systems in several large bodies of granitic rock. The formations are of particular interest to geologists because they record a former climate that was much wetter and more lush than the current dry climate of present-day southern California.

The most popular climbing areas in Joshua Tree are made up of the White Tank monzogranite. Monzogranite, also sometimes called quartz monzonite, is a type of granite composed of quartz, plagioclase feldspar, potassium feldspar, and biotite. Geologists classify the White Tank rock as a monzogranite instead of a granite because it has slightly less quartz than a true granite, so it falls close to the border between the monzonite and granite fields on an igneous rock classification diagram (see figure 4). The White

Tank monzogranite is Cretaceous in age, approximately eighty million years old. The granitic rocks of Yosemite Valley and Tuolumne, as well as many other intrusive rocks in California, formed during the Cretaceous Period. These rocks were all emplaced when there was a convergent boundary along the western coast of California and the floor of the Pacific Ocean, at that time part of the Farallon tectonic plate, subducted beneath the North American plate along an ocean trench. The White Tank monzogranite is extensively exposed throughout the park, including rocks at the Indian Cove, Wonderland of Rocks, Jumbo Rocks, White Tank, and Lost Horse Valley areas.

Joshua Tree is host to several other igneous intrusions, including the Queen Mountain monzogranite, the Oasis monzogranite, the Gold Park diorite, and the Twentynine Palms porphyritic monzogranite. These individual intrusions formed at different locations and different times within the long-lived igneous environment of the North American–Farallon subduction zone. The Oasis monzogranite, which is similar in age to the White Tank rock, is interesting because it contains shiny, silver-colored flecks of muscovite and tiny, dark red nuggets of garnet. The Twentynine Palms intrusion is about 245 million years old and it represents one of the first signals that subduction along western North America had begun. The oldest rocks in Joshua Tree are Precambrian gneisses that make up the "basement" of the exposed crust. These rocks are about 1.7 billion years old.

Like many granite terranes, the rock formations in Joshua Tree were sculpted in a two-stage process that included cracking of the rock along systematic planes and then subsequent chemical erosion of the granite along those planes. It is common in exposures of intrusive igneous rocks to see three sets of fractures, called joints, that are approximately perpendicular to one another. One set forms roughly parallel to the land surface and is called sheeting joints. These fractures form as the rock moves upward in the crust, becomes depressurized, and thus expands. The other two sets are roughly vertical and are at high angles to each other. The origins of these cracks are still debated among geologists, but they likely form from regional tectonic forces that act on the rock as it sits beneath the Earth's surface.

The three joint systems are important because they act as pathways for groundwater to enter the rock. The spacing of these fractures is key to determining the size and shape of the landforms. The rock at Joshua Tree tends to have widely spaced joints, resulting in broad, rounded formations rather than tightly spaced needles.

Climbers on
Houser Buttress
in Joshua Tree
National Park,
California.

PHOTO BY
BRIAN POST

Most of the weathering and erosion of the formations in Joshua Tree occurred during the last ice age (about 100,000 to 10,000 years ago), when Southern California experienced more rainfall than today. In the current dry climate, the formations aren't changing very fast.

Joshua Tree National Park is part of the Transverse Ranges in southern California, a group of highlands so named because they are oriented at an angle to the north-south grain of most of the other features in California. The Transverse Ranges are in their odd orientation because they are being squeezed by the different forces of two tectonic provinces: the transform motion of the San Andreas Fault to the west and the extensional forces of the Basin and Range Province to the east.

References: 9, 63, 79, 139, 140

Why does Tuolumne have all those big crystals?

Rock climbing in Tuolumne has a different feel from climbing down in Yosemite Valley, and it's not just the escape of the crowds and valley walls. The routes themselves are different—more alpine and on slightly different rock. The rock of Tuolumne is part of what geologists call the Tuolumne Intrusive Suite. These are four distinct bodies of granitic rock that have slightly different compositions and different ages but are related nonetheless.

The rocks of the Tuolumne Intrusive Suite include the granodiorite of Kuna Crest (91 million years old); the Half Dome granodiorite (87 million years old); the Cathedral Peak granodiorite (86 million years old); and the Johnson granite porphyry, the youngest intrusion, which has not been directly dated. The Cathedral Peak granodiorite is the unit most climbers are familiar with: It is the largest pluton in the suite and makes up most of the domes we climb in Tuolumne.

The Cathedral Peak granodiorite has what geologists call a porphyritic texture, with large, rectangular crystals surrounded by a matrix of smaller grains. The large crystals in the Cathedral Peak unit are potassium feldspar grains, commonly as large as 2 to 3 inches. Porphyritic texture is the result of the different temperatures at which the different minerals in intrusive rocks crystallize out of magma.

A large body of magma deep in the Earth's crust can take millions of years to solidify into rock. Because minerals crystallize at different temperatures and at different rates, the earliest mineral phases can solidify and float

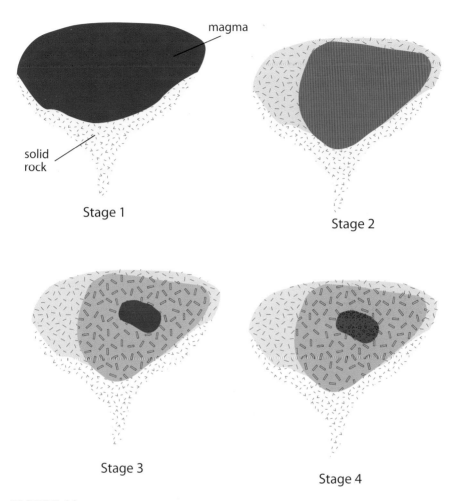

magma

solid
rock

Stage 1

Stage 2

Stage 3

Stage 4

FIGURE 30

*Cross-section view of a large magma chamber cooling in distinct stages, pro-
ducing a nested pattern of related intrusive rocks. This is how the Tuolumne
Intrusive Suite formed. Magma (red and pink regions) along the edges of the
chamber, in contact with the cool country rock, begins to crystallize first. As
minerals crystallize (gray-patterned regions), their chemical components are
removed from the magma and the composition of the magma changes. For this
reason, the rocks that crystallize in the magma chamber change in composition
through time.*

*After complete crystallization of the magma chamber, the region is uplifted
and eroded, exposing the nested pattern of slightly different igneous rocks on
the surface of the Earth. In Tuolumne, erosion of these rock exposures, especially by glaciers, has carved the domes and crags we now enjoy as climbers.*

Ron Kauk climbs The Titanic *(5.12) in* The Needles, *part of the Sierra Nevada Batholith.*

PHOTO BY JIM SURETTE

in the magma as perfect crystals. These crystals can settle to the bottom of a magma chamber due to gravity or become cycled through the chamber along convection currents.

In the case of the Tuolumne Intrusive Suite, geologists believe that a single magma chamber cooled slowly over time, from the outside inward. As the early minerals crystallized during the early stages of cooling along the chamber edges, the removal of these phases changed the composition of the remaining magma. Thus the next stage to cool had a somewhat different composition (see figure 30). This pattern of rock formation causes the different rock types of an intrusive suite to outcrop in a nested, or zoned, pattern.

References: 66, 69

Why is there so much granite in California?

From Joshua Tree to Donner Summit, the eastern spine of California is saturated with bullet-hard, fantastically climbable granite. Technically, it is more correct to call these rocks granitic rocks rather than granite because most of them are not true granites but are related rocks like granodiorite and monzonite (see figure 4). Whatever you call them, these crystalline rocks make up the Sierra Nevada, a mountain range formed from the uplifted roots of volcanoes that were active over 100 million years ago. The granitic rocks are the solidified remnants of huge magma chambers that once fed the active volcanoes. Over time the volcanic highlands were stripped

Jim Surette on the rock of the Sierra Nevada Batholith in The Needles.
PHOTO BY SARAH GARLICK

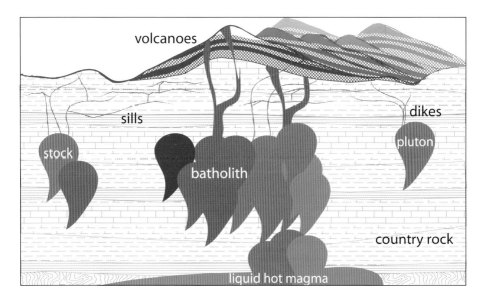

FIGURE 31

Dikes are layers or columns of magma that are oriented at a steep angle (vertical or close to vertical) to the layering of the preexisting host rock, called the country rock. Sills are similar to dikes but are oriented parallel (horizontal or close to horizontal) to the layering of the country rock. Plutons are individual bodies of intrusive igneous rock. Very large (>40 square miles) bodies of intrusive igneous rock are called batholiths, which can be heterogeneous composites of many plutons, as showed here. Small plutons (<40 square miles) are called stocks.

away by erosion. Rivers and glaciers transported the volcanic material particle by particle into the Great Valley, exposing the deep crystalline cores.

The Sierra Nevada Batholith is the technical name of the Sierran granitic rocks. A batholith is simply a very large body of intrusive igneous rock—rock that slowly crystallized out of magma deep in the Earth's crust (see figure 31). The Sierra Nevada Batholith is over 23,000 square miles in area and consists of over 200 individual plutons that were emplaced over about 100 million years. The tectonic environment in which these igneous rocks formed was a continental volcanic arc, similar to the modern-day Andes. In a continental arc, an oceanic plate subducts beneath a continental plate and water driven off of the downgoing plate facilitates partial melting of mantle

What Happened to the Farallon Plate?

The Farallon Plate is the long-lived oceanic plate that was subducted beneath the western boundary of the North American continent during the Mesozoic and early Cenozoic eras (about 200 to 30 million years ago). The Juan de Fuca and Gorda Plates, now subducting beneath the northern boundary of North America, are remnants of the Farallon Plate. Along the California coast, however, the Farallon Plate has disappeared beneath North America, and in its place is a strike-slip margin—the San Andreas Fault—against the adjacent Pacific Plate.

The reorganization of the western North America margin occurred when a mid-oceanic ridge, which is a divergent plate boundary, collided with the subduction zone. The mid-oceanic ridge separated the Farallon Plate from the Pacific Plate to the west, and when it reached the subduction zone, the Farallon Plate disappeared beneath North America.

The merging of the conflicting plate motions of the divergent mid-oceanic ridge and the convergent subduction zone resulted in a shifting of plate motions, causing just enough change to make the North American and Pacific Plates slide past each other instead of converge.

rocks, forming magma. Magma is more buoyant than solid rock and makes its way higher, forming volcanoes at the surface of the Earth and slowly cooling into plutons deeper in the crust.

The granitic rocks of this hundred-million-year-old volcanic arc are exposed today because of uplift of the region and intense erosion. The Great Valley to the west of the Sierra Nevada has provided space for all the rock particles eroded off the Sierra to become deposited. In fact, geologists can look through the package of sediment in the Great Valley and reconstruct the composition of the former volcanic mountains. They call the Great Valley rocks an unroofing sequence, because they record the wearing away of the roof of the mountains.

References: 66, 118, 126

Denali, North America's highest mountain, is made up of granite that is about 60 million years old. It has only been uplifted to the surface in the past 6 million years.

PHOTO BY JIM SURETTE

Northwest and Alaska

Why is Denali the tallest mountain in North America?

At 20,320 feet, Denali, also known as Mount McKinley, is the highest mountain in North America and the crown jewel of the Alaska Range. Other high peaks of the Alaska Range include Mount Foraker, North America's fourth-highest peak (17,400 feet) and Mount Hunter (14,570 feet). These peaks are held up by the hard, granitic rocks of the McKinley sequence, a group of igneous intrusions that crystallized in the Alaskan crust between about 58 and 55 million years ago. The reason these mountains are so tall, however, has to do with the long-lived active tectonic environment of the southern Alaskan margin.

The rocks of Alaska, like those of western Canada and the northwestern U.S., have been assembled by tectonic collisions and volcanic activity along a long-lived convergent plate boundary. Here, the Pacific Plate slides beneath the North American Plate along an oceanic trench. Over time, pieces of island chains, oceanic plateaus, and possibly even small continental fragments have been carried with the oceanic plate to the trench. These rocks are too buoyant to be subducted like regular oceanic crust, so they end up becoming accreted to the North American continental margin (see figure 33).

Contraction along this convergent plate boundary, combined with the addition of new rocks to the North American side, resulted in mountain uplift and thickened crust in the Alaska Range region. In fact, the crust became so thick that the deepest rocks melted. This magma became mixed

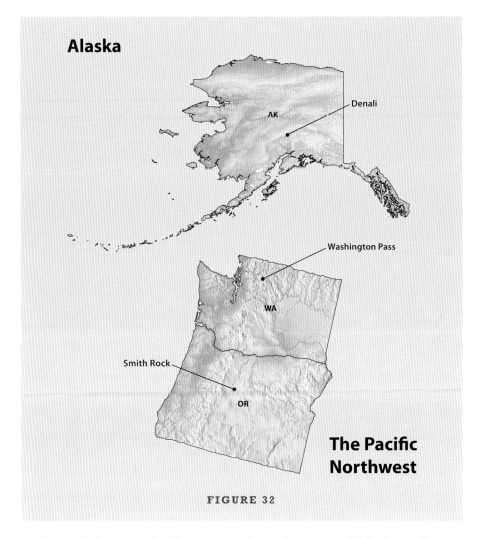

Alaska

Denali

AK

Washington Pass

WA

Smith Rock

OR

The Pacific Northwest

FIGURE 32

with the subduction-related magma and together they solidified into the McKinley sequence of granitic rocks. Above the solidifying granite, volcanic centers may have once existed, but as the tectonic plates continued to converge, the Alaska Range kept uplifting and the volcanoes became eroded down to their crystalline cores. Although the Alaska Range is still uplifting today (rising at a rate of about 1 millimeter per year), the plate boundary has shifted south with the addition of new terranes. The volcanoes of the Wrangell-St. Elias Range and the Aleutian Islands are the present mark of magma rising above the Alaskan subduction zone.

References: 75, 79, 107

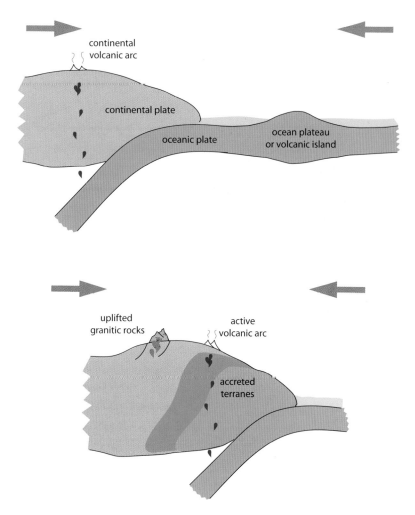

FIGURE 33
Cross-section of southern Alaska showing the tectonic development of the Alaska Range.

What is the Monkey Face at Smith Rock?

The spectacular spires and walls of Oregon's Smith Rock State Park are carved out of 30-million-year-old welded tuff and rhyolite—rocks that formed from the ash explosions and lava flows of an eruptive volcano. Using a map of these rocks and the landscape of the region, geologists have identified a 230-square-mile depression, called a caldera, that is all that is left of this ancient volcano. A caldera is a giant crater that forms when a magma

Just Do It (5.14c), one of the hardest sport climbs in the United States, is part of the Monkey Face, an eroded column of welded tuff in Smith Rock State Park.

PHOTO BY JIM THORNBURG

chamber beneath a volcano erupts a large volume of material. The top of the volcano literally collapses into the newly emptied chamber, creating a huge depression. Smith Rock State Park is on the northwest corner of what is now known as the Crooked River Caldera.

Most of the crags at Smith Rock are made up of welded tuff, a rock that forms when hot ash, sprayed into the atmosphere from a volcanic eruption, settles onto the Earth's surface in a thick sheet, hardening as it cools. Like lava, when ash cools it contracts, sometimes forming giant columns separated by vertical cracks. The Monkey Face at Smith Rock is one of these columns of

hardened ash, now weathered and eroded into its spectacular shape.

The tuff at Smith Rock contains numerous inclusions and fragments, including chunks of hardened rhyolitic lava and pumice and fragments of volcanic glass. Smith Rock State Park also contains formations that are made up of basalt and rhyolite. The rhyolite at Smith Rock is from the same volcano as the welded tuff. Rhyolite is like basalt in that it is an extrusive volcanic rock, formed from lava flows. Rhyolite is different from basalt, though, because it forms from a magma that has less iron and magnesium, resulting in a rock that is less dense and lighter in color. Rhyolite is actually chemically similar to granite, the difference being that granite cools slowly underground, while rhyolite cools quickly after a volcanic eruption of lava. The Shiprock formation, near the Picnic Lunch Wall, is made up of rhyolite. The upper rim of the Crooked River valley at Smith Rock is made up of dark, columnar basalt. The basalt is younger than the welded tuff and rhyolite. It formed at different stages in the last 10 million years—the youngest of which erupted from the Newberry volcano in the Pleistocene, less than one million years ago.

The volcanic activity that created the Smith Rock formations is related to the ongoing volcanic activity of the Cascade Range. The Cascade Range is a volcanic arc—a chain of volcanoes that forms along a subduction zone. Along the Pacific Northwest coastline, the ocean floor is slowly moving toward the continent and sliding beneath it along an ocean trench. Fluids are driven off the down-going oceanic tectonic plate, causing partial melting to occur in the upper mantle, the magma from which rises through the crust and creates volcanoes. The Cascadia subduction zone formed about 36 million years ago and is still active today.

References: 83, 97

Why is there better rock climbing in the North Cascades than in the southern Cascade Range?

Washington Pass, in North Cascades National Park, is host to dozens of long alpine routes, including the 12 pitch classic Liberty Crack on the Liberty Bell. So why is it that splitter routes like Liberty Crack exist in the North Cascades while the southern Cascade Range is dominated by snow and ice climbs? The answer has to do with differences in the geologic histories of the mountains along the length of the greater Cascade and Coast Ranges. The North Cascades are made up of metamorphic and igneous rocks that were faulted and uplifted over millions of years as pieces of volcanic islands, ocean floor, and even continental fragments collided with and became attached to the northwestern margin of North America. This is a similar history to the geology of southern Alaska, and some of the granitic rocks in the North Cascades are analogous to the old, uplifted magma chambers found in the Alaska Range (see figure 33). The southern Cascade Range, however, is an active chain of volcanoes that marks the current volcanic plate boundary of northwestern North America. These are volcanic cones built out of pyroclastic material (ash and debris ejected during a volcanic eruption) and lava flows, neither of which make for very good rock climbing.

The rock at Washington Pass is called the Golden Horn granite, which is about 50 million years old. The Golden Horn granite has a peculiar, sodium-rich chemistry that developed by the mixing of different types of magma. This peculiar chemistry has given rise to unusual minerals in the Golden Horn granite and thus Washington Pass is a popular spot for crystal hunters. Alpine glaciers and frost-action erosion have carved the needles and spires of Washington Pass along joint systems and faults in the granite. These cracks and faults are the bedrock's response to millions of years of active tectonic movement in the Pacific Northwest.

The most adventurous climbers in the Cascades head north of Washington Pass to the Picket Range. The Picket Range is a remote group of jagged peaks that have been carved by small alpine glaciers. Many of the ridges and summits in the Picket Range are made up of a metamorphic rock called hornfels. A hornfels is a metamorphic rock that forms during the extreme heat generated by a large igneous intrusion. The heat from intruding magma bakes the surrounding rock, causing its minerals to recrystallize into tiny interlocking grains. Thus, a hornfels is characterized by having small grains that are welded together into a very hard, dense rock. The hornfels in the Picket Range formed during the intrusion of the underlying Chilliwack Batholith, a group of magmatic rocks that formed during Oligocene–Pliocene time, between about 34 and 5 million years ago.

References: 122a, 134a

The Picket Range in the North Cascades is a remote group of rugged peaks where adventuresome climbers can find solitude and untrammeled rock.
PHOTO BY JOHN BURBIDGE

MacLean Pancoast and guide
on the Marangu Route, Mount
Kilimanjaro, Tanzania.
PHOTO BY BRIAN POST

10

Africa

Is Kilimanjaro going to blow its top?

Tanzania's Mount Kilimanjaro is one of the most popular peaks to climb in Africa. At 19,340 feet elevation, Kilimanjaro has the distinction of being the highest freestanding mountain in the world. Kilimanjaro is a stratovolcano, a type of volcano that is constructed out of thick layers of ash and lava and is characterized by steep sides and violent eruptions. The shape and violent eruptions of stratovolcanoes develop because of the highly viscous nature of their lava.

There are three distinct volcanic cones on Kilimanjaro: Kibo, the highest; Shira, the oldest and most westerly; and Mawenzi, the easternmost cone. The overlapping flows of these three vents have created the single volcanic mountain of Kilimanjaro. Kilimanjaro is less than a million years old and still contains magma in its depths. However, the volcano is technically listed as being inactive, or dormant, and there have been no known eruptions in recent history.

Kilimanjaro is part of the East African Rift (see figure 34)—a zone of continental extension, where the African continent is tearing apart, in the early stages of forming a new ocean basin. The East African Rift is part of a triple junction of tectonic plates between the African, Arabian, and Indian Plates. The Arabian Plate, carrying Saudi Arabia, is moving away from the African Plate, and in the process, opening the Red Sea.

References: 17, 128

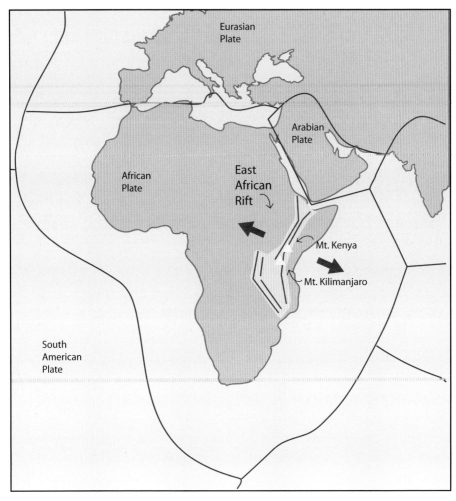

FIGURE 34
Map of the tectonic environment of Africa. The East African Rift is the beginning of a new plate boundary.

Why are there sandstone boulders in Rocklands, South Africa?

Rocklands, a South African bouldering area that has gained some attention from the climbing media in the past few years, is part of the Cederberg Mountains, located about 125 miles north of Cape Town. The Cederberg Mountains are part of what geologists call the Cape Fold Belt, a region of folded and faulted sedimentary rock that formed during tectonic contraction within a sedimentary basin. The contraction that forced up the Cape Fold Belt occurred during the assembly of the supercontinent Pangaea during the

The Cederberg Mountains in South Africa host boulders and crags made up of 480- to 430-million-year-old sandstone of the Table Mountain Group.

PHOTO BY
MAJKA BURHARDT

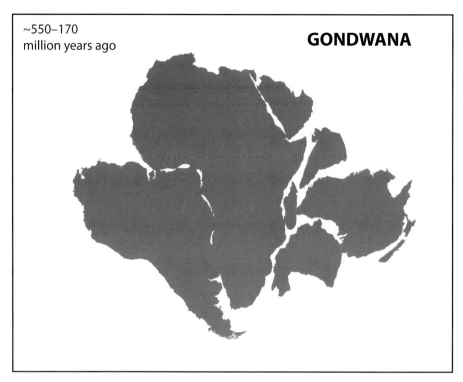

FIGURE 35

late Paleozoic and early Mesozoic eras, about 300 million years ago. This was the same large-scale event that put the finishing touches on the Appalachian Mountains, as well as built the Ural Mountains in Europe, the Atlas Mountains in North Africa, and the Ellsworth Mountains in Antarctica.

The rocks that were folded and thrust into the Cape Fold Belt uplifts are made up of thick sequences of sediment that were deposited on the tectonically quiet edge of the African continent between the late Cambrian and the Carboniferous periods, about 500 to 330 million years ago. These sedimentary rocks are called the Cape Supergroup. The boulders at Rocklands are sandstone from the Table Mountain Group of the Cape Supergroup. The Table Mountain Group is a sequence of Ordovician to early Silurian (about 480 to 430 million years old) sandstones and thin bands of shale, and it represents one of the thickest accumulations of quartz sand on Earth.

The Table Mountain sandstone is made up of rounded grains of quartz sand that were deposited in a shallow marine or beach setting. Geologists think that the extraordinarily thick accumulation of these rounded quartz sands means there must have been severe chemical weathering during this time to produce such pure and rounded grains. Perhaps this was due to an unusually corrosive atmosphere at that time—an atmosphere higher in carbon dioxide because of widespread volcanism is one idea.

The Table Mountain Group is also important because it records a very early period of glaciation on Earth, right at the Ordovician-Silurian boundary, about 440 million years ago. This record is in the form of glacial deposits within the sedimentary sequence. Geologists have found similar-aged glacial deposits in other continents and have used these rocks to reconstruct the long-lived continent called Gondwana, comprising South America, Australia, Antarctica, New Zealand, Arabia, and India (see figure 35). This supercontinent formed sometime between 550 and 500 million years ago, and its development led to the uplift of mountains that were the source region for the Table Mountain Group sediments.

References: 141, 131

The low, steep cliff band toward the bottom of this photograph is the famous Yellow Band on Mount Everest. The Yellow Band is a sequence of metamorphosed limestone that originated in the ocean off the north coast of India, before India collided with Asia to form the Himalaya.

PHOTO BY JIM SURETTE

11

Asia

What is the Yellow Band on Mount Everest?

One of the most distinctive features of Mount Everest, besides its height, is a section of yellowish-orange layered rocks near the peak's summit. This section of rocks is called the Yellow Band, and it lies between 26,900 and 27,800 feet on the mountain, representing one of the last obstacles Everest climbers have to tackle on their push between Camp III and Camp IV on the *Southeast Ridge* route.

The Yellow Band is a sequence of layered marble, essentially metamorphosed limestone, that is yellowish in color due to the chemical weathering of calcium carbonate. The Yellow Band rocks are Ordovician in age (approximately 450 million years old) and are the remnants of a shallow ocean platform that once lay to the north of the Indian subcontinent before it collided with Asia to form the Himalaya. In a sense, the Yellow Band captures one of the best examples of Earth's tectonic cycling of rocks. The Yellow Band rocks, once marine sediments deposited below sea level, were thrust skyward to the upper flanks of the world's highest mountains by the forces of Earth's tectonic plates. Now the Yellow Band oceanic rocks are being eroded off the high faces of the mountains, and their components are being recycled back down to the oceans, transported by the movement of glaciers and river systems.

The geologic structure of Mount Everest is not exactly simple. The upper reaches of the mountain are cut by two large fault systems, the Qomolangma and Lhotse Detachments (see figure 36). The Qomolangma Detachment separates the Yellow Band from the summit rocks of Everest, which

145

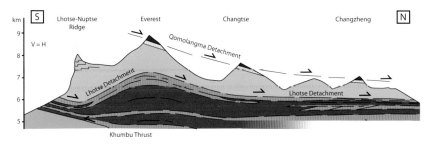

FIGURE 36

Cross-section diagram of Mount Everest and surrounding mountains. Diagram from Searle et al., 2003 (reference 114). Used with permission from M. P. Searle.

are unmetamorphosed limestones that contain fragments of coral. Geologists do not know how much displacement has taken place along this fault, but the different layering orientations of the summit limestones and the Yellow Band marble are evidence that the fault exits. Below the Yellow Band is a series of thin-bedded dark shales that are called the Everest Series. Below the Everest Series is the Lhotse Detachment, a fault that separates the Everest Series from underlying gneisses and granitic intrusions that make up a rock unit known as the Greater Himalaya Slab. These are hard, crystalline rocks that originated deep in the Earth's crust and have been brought up to the Earth's surface by the continued tectonic movement of the Himalayan Mountain system. The steep Kangshung east face of Everest is held up by the hard granitic rocks of the Greater Himalaya Slab.

Why is there so much granite in Pakistan?

If you're into alpine rock climbing, you've probably had daydreams of the granite towers of the Baltoro Glacier in Pakistan's Karakoram Range. But have you ever wondered why those towers are in such a difficult-to-get-to place? Why aren't the Trango Towers, say, in New Hampshire? One of the main reasons is that everything in the Himalaya is big—all the other collisional mountain belts on Earth are old and eroded, while the Himalaya is still actively building. Another important factor is alpine glaciation. The combination of the tectonic uplift of hard, granitic rock and the sculpting power of glaciers produces the famously high, steep towers.

The backbone of the Karakoram is made up of a huge batholith of granitic intrusions, one of which is the Baltoro granite. The Baltoro granite is

Great Trango Tower, in Pakistan, is a spire made up of the Baltoro granite.

PHOTO BY JIM SURETTE

A Short History of the Himalaya

The Himalaya Range is the world's most dramatic example of continent-to-continent collisions. The collision began about 50 million years ago when India, on a fast northward track from its former location near Australia and Antarctica, plowed into the southern margin of Asia. Today India is still moving northward relative to Asia, and the Himalayan system is still very active.

The Himalayan Mountains are the result of contraction and shortening in the Earth's crust along this collisional boundary. The Himalayan chain is important not only because it hosts the world's tallest mountains but also because it influences global climate patterns and provides fresh water to all of Southeast Asia. For geologists these mountains are the archetypal example by which we understand large-scale tectonic collisions in the past.

As you might suspect, the Himalaya is not as simple as a welt of upthrust rock in a collision zone. When you look in detail, you see that there were other rocks caught up in the collision, like pieces of oceanic basins and oceanic island chains. Also, the tectonic forces in the Himalayan crust are not simply all contractional as one might expect in a collisional zone. Large strike-slip faults and extensional faults have developed around and within the Tibetan Plateau and possibly have even crossed into the Himalayan front.

One of the more interesting questions of Himalayan geology is how the deep granitic rocks that hold up the Himalayan high peaks made it to the Earth's surface. These rocks formed relatively deep in the crust during the continental collision, so why are they now exposed on the mountains' upper flanks? The favored explanation is that the Himalayan crust has become so overly thickened that some of its rocks have partially melted, forming a weakened zone in the middle crust. This weak, partially melted layer has been squeezed like toothpaste up to the Earth's surface along large, regional fault systems.

References: 112, 114

about 21 million years old. It formed when the enormously thick crust of the Himalaya started to melt in its deeper regions. Continued uplift of the Himalaya has brought this granite up to the surface, where its vertical fractures have been exploited by scouring glaciers and wind, carving the granite into steep spires and peaks.

References: 50, 100

Why do Thailand's coastal cliffs have such incredible overhanging routes?

The ocean-side limestone cliffs of Railay Beach are one of the world's most spectacular examples of erosion by ocean waves. Geologists call this wave-action erosion, and it is one of the most important processes that have shaped the western coast of Thailand. This coast is exposed to the Andaman Sea, which is a high-energy erosive environment during the monsoon months of April to September. The waves affect low-lying exposures of limestone bedrock, causing undermining of the cliffs and rock fall, which further steepens the topography.

The Railay Beach area is an example of what geologists call karst landscape. Karst landscape is the evolution of the land by the dissolution of limestone bedrock that occurs in humid climates. Over time, water dissolves limestone, rounding it into towers and conelike forms, as well as smaller scale features like runnels and tufas. All of these features are found in this region of Thailand.

The limestone at Railay Beach is part of the Ratburi Group, which is Permian in age, or about 300 to 250 million years old. During the Permian, most of the Earth's continents were joined together in the supercontinent Pangaea. Parts of Southeast Asia, including parts of the Thai Peninsula, Indonesia, and China, however, were part of a chain of continental fragments that were separated from Pangaea during the Permian. This long chain of land, located near the equator, was ideal for the growth of huge networks of coral reefs. These ancient reefs are now the Permian-age limestones that are common all across Southeast Asia.

References: 35, 61, 62

Australia's Grampians National Park is home to massive walls of quartz-rich sandstones that are about 450 million years old. The Grampians sandstone is almost 100% quartz, and it has been slightly metamorphosed, making the rock very strong and hard.

PHOTO BY JIM SURETTE

Australia
and New Zealand

What are the Grampians?

Australia's Grampians National Park lies west of Melbourne, in Victoria. The Grampian Mountains, preserved in the park, comprise a group of strike ridges—landforms created by the shallow dip of tilted, resistant sedimentary layers. The rock of the Grampians is a very thick sequence of quartz sandstones, called the Grampians Group, which was deposited in shallow marine waters and river deltas in Silurian time, about 450 million years ago. These sedimentary rocks were thickened, folded, and tilted during development of a fold-and-thrust belt called the Lachlan Fold Belt about 430 million years ago. The Lachlan Fold Belt developed during contraction along a subduction zone that existed around the entire margin of Gondwana, a supercontinent that included all of the landmasses of the present-day Southern Hemisphere (see figure 35).

References: 24, 49

Why aren't there more mountains in Australia?

Australia is one of the oldest continental landmasses on Earth and also one of the most isolated. In its long lifetime, Australia has experienced a relatively quiet tectonic history and has never developed any large mountain belts. The Australian continent was initially assembled during the early Precambrian, over 2 billion years ago. Much of Australia's geologic history,

Andrew Dunbar climbs the ancient sandstone of the Grampians National Park in Victoria, Australia.

PHOTO BY
JIM SURETTE

including all of the Paleozoic era (about 540 to 250 million years ago) and much of the Mesozoic Era (about 250 to 100 million years ago), took place while it was tectonically sheltered within the supercontinent Gondwana (see figure 35). The last major tectonic episode to affect Australia was the breakup of Gondwana, which started around 170 million years ago.

Presently, Australia is relatively isolated from other continents, especially on its east, west, and south coasts, which are all passive margins. On its north coast, however, the Australian plate is moving northward and colliding with the various microplates of Southeast Asia. This plate boundary is complicated, though, and it lies far outboard enough that the effects of this collision have not yet been felt on the continent itself.

References: 15, 140

Why are the boulders at Castle Hill, New Zealand, such interesting shapes? Why aren't they just round?

New Zealand's Castle Hill bouldering area gained worldwide attention when it was featured in Mike Call's 2002 climbing film, *Frequent Flyers*. The high density of interesting boulder formations and cool-looking problems instantly put the Castle Hill–Canterbury area on the map of international bouldering destinations. The area is also a popular tourist spot on the South Island hiking circuit and has been the filming location for several Hollywood films. The rocks that give Castle Hill such a distinctive look are rounded blocks of limestone, shaped into strange-looking formations by the dissolving action of groundwater. This is called karst landscape, which develops anywhere limestone is exposed in a humid environment.

The Castle Hill basin itself is a downdropped block of land formed by motion along the steep faults that created the surrounding Torlesse and Craigieburn Ranges. The Castle Hill Basin is actually a small sub-basin of the greater Canterbury Basin. The Canterbury Basin originated about 80 million years ago when New Zealand rifted away from western Antarctica. Before rifting, New Zealand was part of Gondwana, a continent comprising Antarctica, Australia, and India that formed the Southern Hemisphere portion of the supercontinent Pangaea. The breakup of Gondwana created a passive margin on the eastern side of New Zealand, resulting in the deposition of a thick sequence of sedimentary rocks, including limestone.

The limestone at Castle Hill is Oligocene in age, about 30 million years old. These limestones represent the maximum transgression, or rise in sea level, in the Canterbury Basin group of passive margin sediments.

References: 78, 94

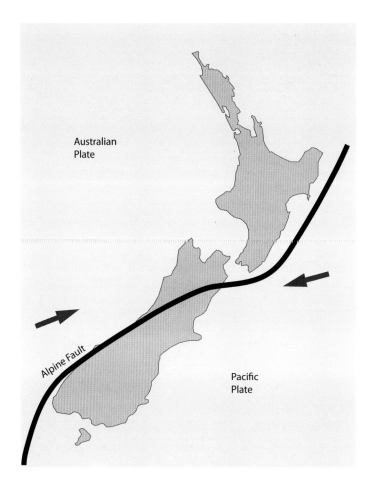

FIGURE 37
New Zealand has the distinction of being one of the few countries that is cut down the middle by a tectonic boundary. The Alpine Fault is a transform boundary, separating the Indo-Australian Plate to the west from the Pacific Plate to the east.

New Zealand: Two Tectonic Plates

The South Island of New Zealand is one of the few continental landmasses on Earth that sits astride two tectonic plates (see figure 37). It is part of the Pacific Plate to the east and the Indo-Australian Plate to the west. The boundary between these two plates is the Alpine Fault, a huge structure that controls the entire topography of the South Island. Motion along the Alpine Fault is a combination of strike-slip and convergence. The main part of the South Island, on the east side of the Alpine Fault, is moving southward with respect to the west side of the island, but it is also moving toward it, causing the Pacific Plate to be thrust up over the Australian Plate. This thrusting has caused uplift of the Southern Alps, which include Mount Cook. The Southern Alps are still being uplifted today at a rate of about 7 millimeters per year, and earthquakes are common along the Alpine Fault.

13

Antarctica

What type of rock makes up Mount Vinson, the tallest mountain in Antarctica? How did the mountain form?

At 16,050 feet, Mount Vinson, is the tallest mountain in Antarctica and thus one of the "seven summits"—the highest points on each of the seven continents. But Mount Vinson has more in common with the boulders of South Africa than any of the other seven summits. Mount Vinson is located within the Ellsworth Mountains in Antarctica. This range is made up entirely of sedimentary strata that were laid down along the tectonically quiet coastline of Antarctica between about 300 and 500 million years ago. During this time, Antarctica was part of the supercontinent Gondwana, which also included Australia, New Zealand, Antarctica, Arabia, and India (see figure 35). The Cape Supergroup sedimentary rocks of South Africa—including the Table Mountain sandstone of Rocklands and Table Mountain—are similar in age and type to the Ellsworth rocks, probably reflecting their similar position along the edge of Gondwana. Like the Cape Supergroup, the sedimentary rocks of the Ellsworth Mountains were folded and thrust into mountains during the formation of Pangaea about 250 million years ago.

Reference: 31

A teenage Jim Surette samples the limestone at Buoux on Chouca (5.13c).
PHOTO BY NEIL CANNON

14

Europe

Why does Europe have so much limestone?

The Verdon, Ceuse, Buoux, El Chorro, Rodellar, Siurana: The list of famous European limestone climbing destinations goes on and on. Europe's endowment in steep sport climbing cliffs goes back over 200 million years, to a time when much of the world's landmasses were trapped in the supercontinent Pangaea. As Pangaea rifted apart, new oceans were created and, with them, new shorelines on the edges of the individual continents. A new shoreline developed along the northern coast of Africa, as well as along the southern coast of Europe. The ocean that separated these landmasses was called Tethys.

The closing of the Tethys Ocean as Africa moved northward, eventually to collide with the southern coast of Europe, has fundamentally shaped the geology and landscape of Europe. Most of the limestones found in Europe originated in the Tethys Ocean. Tethys was centered near the equator, where temperatures were relatively warm, and it stayed shallow for much of its existence. Warm temperatures and shallow seas are the two main requirements for the growth of coral reefs, which eventually become limestone. Thick limestone beds were deposited in Tethys throughout the Cretaceous period (about 140 to 65 million years ago).

This limestone became caught up in the building of the Alps during the collision of the African and European Plates. The Alps contain the remnants of two passive continental margins and an intervening ocean basin, which are all regions dominated by marine sediments.

JB Tribout climbing Europe's famous Cretaceous (140–65 million years old) limestone.
PHOTO BY JIM SURETTE

The African and European Plates started to collide during the early Tertiary, about 50 million years ago. Contraction during this tectonic collision resulted in faulting and folding of thick sheets of sedimentary rock, much of which was marine. The combination of faulting and folding of thick sheets on top of one another sometimes doubled or even tripled sedimentary sequences, increasing the amount of limestone even more. The collision continued until the Pliocene, about 4 million years ago.

Reference: 101

What are those brainlike, sloping textures of the Fontainebleau boulders?

Fontainebleau, in the Paris Basin, is a world-class example of polygonally cracked sandstone. Networks of fine cracks, forming polygons that are dominantly hexagonal, create the intricate surface textures of which Fontaine-

Kelley Greenwald sticks to the sandstone slopers of Fontainebleau. The patterned rock in the foreground is called polygonal cracking.
PHOTO BY ANNE SKIDMORE

bleau is renowned. The sandstone is early Oligocene (about 36 to 27 million years old) in age and is part of a sedimentary unit that is over 200 feet thick. The Fontainebleau sandstone is fine grained and almost entirely composed of quartz. It rests on top of shale and is overlain by limestone. The Paris Basin formed during the continental collisions that brought together the supercontinent Pangaea, and it has been the locus of accumulating sedimentary rocks since the Triassic, about 220 million years ago.

Polygonal cracking like you see at Fontainebleau can be found all across the globe on many different rock types. The origins of polygonal cracking on the surfaces of rock formations are not entirely understood. One of the leading hypotheses is that it has to do with the formation of surface crusts on the rock. These crusts could be more susceptible to tensile stresses affecting the rock, causing surface cracking; the crusts themselves could shrink when they form; or they could be more susceptible to periods of wetting and drying that also cause shrinkage and thus cracking. At Fontainebleau, the surface polygons are notably regular and are between 3 and 5 inches in diameter. The crack spacing and polygon size are functions of the rock strength and amount of stress that formed them.

Surface crusts are formed by the precipitation of minerals or salts on the surface or in the uppermost pore spaces of a rock formation. At Fontainebleau the surface crusts are silica cement, which some geologists think may have once been a gel that oozed out of the rock onto the surface and then hardened.

References: 57, 136

Why is the Eiger falling down?

The famous limestone of the Eiger, part of the Swiss Alps, is becoming more famous in recent years for its rock fall. A huge slab of rock, over 800 feet wide and long, on the northeastern face of the Eiger collapsed on July 13, 2006. The slide occurred because of the retreat of the Lower Grindelwald Glacier. The glacier was at its maximum extent in the late nineteenth century, when it reached the bottom of the scar of the recent landslide. Geologists think that the glacier was like a buttress, and when it retreated, the rock slab started to "fatigue," or detach from the wall. General warming— warmer summers and winters—in the European Alps are disturbing the permafrost that usually keeps the loose rocks bonded.

The limestone of the Eiger is Jurassic in age (about 200 to 150 million years old), and it overlies older crystalline rocks (gneisses, schists, and granites) that make up the adjacent Monch and Jungfrau Peaks. These mountains are part of a large sheet of rocks called the Helvetic Nappe that formed during the uplift of the Alps.

Reference: 95

What kind of rock is gritstone?

Gritstones, or grits, are coarse-grained rocks that are used as millstones in flour mills. For climbers, though, gritstone refers to a very hard, compact sandstone that forms crags and cliffs in the Pennine Uplands and the Peak District of England. This rock is the Millstone grit—a late Carboniferous (about 300 million years old) sandstone that is interbedded with shales and overlies limestones. The sandstones are notably rich in feldspars and are thus characterized as subarkosic or even arkosic. The rocks are very hard and impervious for sandstones, and they are more resistant to weathering than surrounding rocks. Their resistant nature, especially compared with underlying and overlying limestones and shales, is the reason why these rocks are cliff-formers in this region.

Reference: 110

La Esfinge is a granite big wall in Peru's Cordillera Blanca. The granite of the Cordillera Blanca has been uplifted to the surface by the active tectonics of the region.
PHOTO BY SARAH GARLICK

15

South America

Why are the Andes so high?

Alpine climbers and mountaineers know that you don't have to go to the Himalaya to get high-altitude climbing experience. From Cotopaxi (19,347 feet) and Chimborazo (20,561 feet) in Ecuador to Tolima (17,110 feet) in Colombia, Illampu (21,276 feet) in Bolivia, Huascarán (22,205 feet) in Peru, and Aconcagua (22,834 feet) in Argentina, there are high-altitude adventures to be had throughout the South American continent. These peaks are part of the greater Andean Cordillera, also known as the Andes, which stretches over 3,000 miles along the western coast of South America.

The Andes are the modern archetypal example of a mountain range produced during the convergence between an oceanic plate and a continental plate. Here the dense, oceanic Nazca Plate slides eastward beneath the buoyant, continental South American Plate along an oceanic trench (see figure 38). Fluids are driven off the downgoing oceanic plate as it experiences higher pressures and temperatures, causing partial melting in the overlying mantle rocks. This melting leads to a chain of volcanoes in the continental plate above the subduction zone, known as a volcanic arc. The Andes are a continental volcanic arc. However, the high peaks of the Andes are not simply tall volcanoes, as is commonly believed. Instead, the Andes are primarily constructed by structural thickening of the crust by tectonic contraction and shortening. It is on top of this thickened crust that the classic subduction-related volcanoes are built.

The subduction zone along the western edge of South America has been active continuously since Jurassic time, so roughly during the past

FIGURE 38

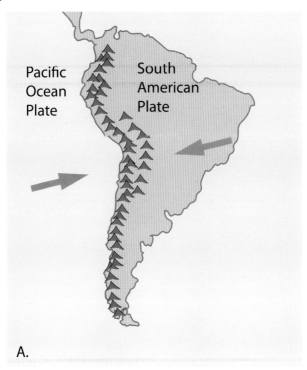

A. Map of South America showing the length of the Andean mountain chain and the convergence between the South American and Pacific tectonic plates.

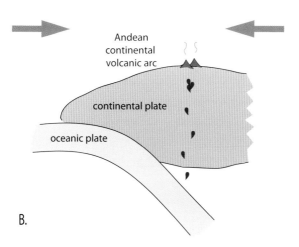

B. Cross-section showing the subduction of the Pacific Plate beneath the South American Plate, generating the volcanoes of South America.

200 million years. During this time, however, the rate and the angle of subduction and plate convergence have changed considerably and have had important effects on the geology of South America. Right now, the oceanic Nazca Plate is sliding beneath South America at a rate of approximately 4 inches per year. Most of the high peaks of the Andes we see today were formed only in the last 30 million years. This topography is the result of structural thickening of the crust by faulting and folding, as well as uplift of the crust by an underlying hot region of mantle, in addition to the accumulation of volcanic rocks.

References: 2, 56

How is the Cordillera Blanca like the Sierra Nevada?

The Cordillera Blanca, with more than 200 summits over 16,000 feet, is host to the highest mountains in Peru, including Huascaran (22,205 feet). These high peaks are made up of the Cordillera Blanca Batholith, a huge body of granodiorite that is about 8 million years old. This is one of the youngest exposed bodies of granitic rock in the world. The Cordillera Blanca Batholith was emplaced in a similar manner to the Sierra Nevada Batholith of California: by the generation and solidification of granitic magma deep in the Earth's crust above a subduction zone. Also like the Sierra Nevada, the upper volcanoes that were fed by this magma have been stripped away, or unroofed, uplifting and exposing their crystalline cores in the form of granitic mountains. But unlike the Sierra Nevada, the subduction zone off the coast of Peru is still active today.

The reason the Cordillera Blanca Batholith has been uplifted to the Earth's surface has to do with the oceanic plate that is being subducted down an oceanic trench along the west coast of Peru. Geologists think that a mid-ocean spreading ridge—a zone of young, hot oceanic crust was subducted into the trench, causing the uplift of the Cordilla Blanca. Hot rocks are more buoyant than old, cold crust, so the subducted slab of young oceanic crust may have risen underneath the continent in what is called flat-slab subduction. The rise of the oceanic slab triggered uplift in the continental crust, which was already weak from all that magma. Uplift along detachment faults (see figure 25) then brought the granitic rocks to the Earth's surface. If you've ever climbed in the Cordillera Blanca, you've probably noticed the unique orientation of the range—with a long, north-south flatland

FIGURE 39
How Joint Patterns Influence Landforms

A. Photograph of Cerro Torre and surrounding peaks in southern Argentina's Los Glaciares National Parque. PHOTO BY KIRSTEN KREMER

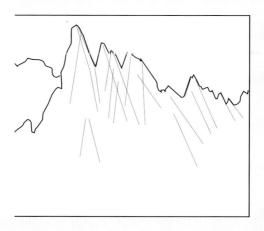

B. Line drawing of Cerro Torre with joint systems traced in red. Notice the two distinct orientations of the joints and how they correspond to the mountain morphology.

next to the mountains and east-west trending valleys, or quebradas, accessing the different peaks. The north-south flank of the range is the Cordillera Blanca detachment fault. The east-west quebradas are deeply incised valleys, indicating active land uplift and downcutting by rivers. The mountains are

C. Photograph of the Fitz Roy massif in southern Argentina's Los Glaciares National Parque. PHOTO BY JIM SURETTE

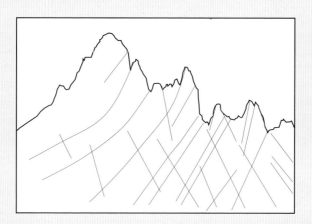

D. Line drawing of Fitz Roy with joint systems traced in red. Notice the two distinct orientations of the joints and how they correspond to the mountain morphology.

still rising at a rate of about 1 millimeter per year, activity that causes earthquakes like the one in 1970 that devastated the town of Yungay.

Reference: 88

FIGURE 40
How Cracks Form

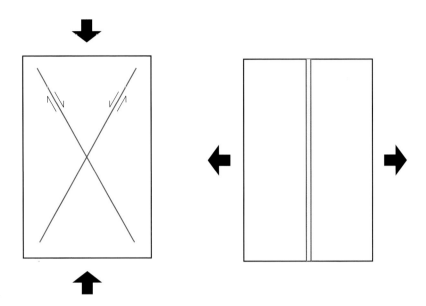

A. Compression forces result in two orientations of fractures, called conjugate shear fractures.

B. Tension forces result in cracks opening perpendicular to the direction of tension.

Why is Cerro Torre so slender?

Cerro Torre, the striking ice-plastered tower in Argentine Patagonia, has one of the world's most coveted alpine summits. One of the reasons Cerro Torre has inspired so much attention by climbers is its extreme needlelike form. Cerro Torre's shape is a dramatic example of rock needle formation in crystalline rocks by erosion along steeply oriented joint surfaces. In fact, the orientation and high density of joints shape all of the peaks in the Fitz Roy Group, which is why there are so many different spires in the region (see figure 39). The joints in the Fitz Roy Group tend to be aligned in two orientations that are at an angle to each other. These are called conjugate systems, and they are common in many different rock types and regions. The origins of conjugate and perpendicular fracture systems are still topics of research and debate among geologists. Conjugate fracture systems develop in the laboratory when you place a material under compression (see figure 40). But most rock joints are believed to be cracks that open under tension, not compression, and tension cracks only form in one orientation, perpendicular to the direction of extension. To explain the conjugate and perpendicular joint systems, geologists have suggested that the multiple systems are tension cracks that formed at different times, under changing tectonic conditions. Others have suggested that a single compressional tectonic event could cause the fractures, and the fractures could open into cracks by weathering and erosion over time.

Cerro Torre and the other peaks in the Fitz Roy Group are part of the Fitz Roy pluton—a body of granitic rock about 18 million years old that is considered to be related to several other granitic intrusions in southern Patagonia, including the Torres del Paine pluton. These granitic intrusions likely formed due to melting in the thickened crust of the southern Andes. There was a reorganization of the tectonic plates here during the same time, which may also have influenced the generation of these granite intrusions.

Cerro Torre is one of the world's most coveted alpine summits.
PHOTO BY JIM SURETTE

References: 3, 29, 126

Anne Skidmore climbs
Recompense (5.9) on
Cathedral Ledge,
New Hampshire.
PHOTO BY JIM SURETTE

General Rock Questions

Are there any geology tips for finding a new crag?

If you're motivated to find new rock, you might consider borrowing a few tools from geologists to aid in your search: geologic maps and aerial photographs. Geologic maps are exactly what they sound like—maps of geology. Using colors or symbols to differentiate rock types, a typical geologic map shows bedrock type superimposed on topography. A climber could use a geologic map to find his or her favorite rock type—granite, for example— and then search the topographic contour lines for areas within a granite formation that show steep topography. I have heard of alpine climbers searching for unclimbed granite spires in the Himalaya using this technique. The U.S. Geological Survey (USGS) has an online database of geologic maps for the United States: http://ngmdb.usgs.gov. You can also browse the USGS publications list and their store for access to worldwide geologic maps: www .usgs.gov. Other tools that could be helpful in your search are aerial photographs and satellite images. In this age of Google Earth and Google Maps, these tools are no longer the domain of ivory-tower scientists and government agencies. Use the rock-type and topographic information you dig up on the geologic maps and cross-reference it with aerial or satellite images to see if there are climbable landforms like cliff bands, caves, or boulder fields. If Google doesn't come through for you, try the USGS collection of aerial photographs: www.usgs.gov/pubprod/aerial.html.

What is the difference between a rock and a mineral?

In a simple sense, minerals are the building blocks of rocks and rocks are the building blocks of our Earth. So then, you might ask, what are the building blocks of minerals? Minerals are made up of elements—either single elements like gold (Au) or chemical compounds like quartz (SiO_2). But not all elements on the periodic table form minerals. An element or compound also has to obey the following rules in order to be classified as a mineral: (1) It must be naturally occurring; (2) it can't be or ever have been alive; and (3) it must have a crystalline form. Rocks, then, are naturally occurring aggregates of minerals. Quartzite, for example, is a rock that is made up of many grains of the mineral quartz. Granite is a rock that is made up of the minerals quartz, feldspar, and usually hornblende or mica.

What is the best type of rock for working slopers, stemming, slab climbing, off-widthing, crimping, and underclinging?

Are there correlations between specific climbing movements and rock types? The answer is yes . . . and no. Many rock features, like cracks, pockets, and corners, are found in a variety of different kinds of rock. But some rock types and environmental conditions will lead to certain features more commonly than others. Basalt, for example, can form groups of hexagonal columns as it cools, forming excellent stemming corners and vertical cracks. Granite landforms are often dome shaped and are thus ideal for slab climbing. Slopers form where rock edges or corners become rounded, usually by processes of chemical weathering. Chemical weathering can be enhanced if rocks are exposed or even partially buried by soil in relatively warm, wet environments. Off-widths and other wide cracks can form by the weathering of rock fractures over long periods of time. Crimpers and underclings can form on the edges of bedding planes or on the edges of fractures that have not opened into cracks. The fine layering, or foliation, of mica schist and gneiss also forms great crimpers and edges.

Why are some climbing areas more polished than others?

Rock faces that are exposed to moving ice or water for long timescales will usually become polished. The process can take hundreds or even thousands of years, but in the same way a rock tumbler will polish a pebble, a stream or glacier carrying grit will put a shine on a landform.

In landscapes that are shaped by glaciers, the direction of ice flow determines which rock faces become polished and which rock faces become broken or pitted by ice plucking (see figure 6). Polish occurs where fine rock particles in the ice rub against the bedrock as the glacier moves. If the glacial ice is carrying larger chunks of rock instead, the bedrock will become carved with rough grooves, called striations, in the direction of ice flow. The best polish develops where streams of meltwater underneath glaciers pass across bedrock. These glacial streams are choked with the ultrafine rock dust that comes from the pulverizing action of the glacier. (These particles are what give glacier-fed rivers their intense blue color instead of being clear.) Moving across a rock surface, the dust acts as polishing grit.

Rock polish can also develop by nonglacial streams. Any moving water that carries a sediment load can scour bedrock, if it is exposed. Polish can even develop by wind in areas where blowing sand is common. However, this phenomenon is usually seen only on small pebbles on windblown surfaces in the desert.

Why is some granite more crumbly than other granite?

Have you ever been climbing in an area of granitic rock and noticed that the rock of some routes is more crumbly than others? Or perhaps you've avoided certain routes or areas because the guidebook uses the words "kitty litter" in their description? Crumbly or kitty-litter granite has its unfortunate texture because of a process known as granular disintegration. Granular disintegration is one of the most common styles of granite weathering and usually develops in areas where moisture is able to penetrate the rock.

Shady areas or areas that hold standing water will be more susceptible to granular disintegration. Granite is typically an impermeable rock, and many granitic surfaces will be relatively unchanged by the presence of water for long time periods. But once a surface becomes permeable because of cracks or fissures, weathering can take hold and progress relatively quickly. This is why there is often an abrupt boundary between disintegrating and solid granite.

How does desert varnish form?

If you're a desert rat, it doesn't get much better than a rope-stretching splitter up bullet-hard, chocolate-colored sandstone. But have you ever reached the top of a desert pitch and found that the smooth, solid rock you'd been jamming had turned into a sand-colored, friable mess? The change likely happened when you climbed from a section of sandstone with desert varnish to a section of rock with little or no varnish.

Desert varnish, also known as rock varnish, is a patina, or surface coating, that commonly develops on rocks in arid environments (although it can develop in humid climates as well). Climbers tend to think of it as a feature of sandstone, but desert varnish can develop on any rock type, including limestone and granite. Desert varnish is a hard, dark crust that is usually less than 0.5 millimeter thick. It is composed of clay minerals, manganese oxide, and iron oxide. It's the manganese and iron that produce the color of desert varnish more manganese gives varnish a black, shiny, metallic look; more iron leads to a lighter, red- or brown-tinted varnish.

The question of how desert varnish forms is one that has been hotly debated since the days of Charles Darwin. We know that desert varnish is not simply a surface crust where components of the host rock are dissolved away or concentrated, because the composition of desert varnish is the same on host rocks of different compositions. Most scientists think that the clay minerals in desert varnish originate as airborne dust particles that are transported to the rock's surface by wind and water. The big question lies with the manganese and iron oxides—chemical components that are common by-products of bacterial metabolism. Do these components require the help of microscopic bacteria living on or just beneath the surface of the rock to form? Or can they be produced inorganically?

As of 2006, many scientists consider the mystery of desert varnish to be solved. A London paleontologist, Randall Perry, determined that the composition of desert varnish is actually mostly silica and that the amounts of manganese and iron are less than previously thought. Silica has nonbiologic origins, and it reaches the surface of a rock either by atmospheric dust or by the leaching of chemical compounds from the rock's interior. The exciting part of Perry's work is his discovery that as desert varnish forms, it acts like a sticky fly strip, trapping any detritus that falls, lands, or walks across the surface of a rock. This detritus may include fragments of ancient life. These fragments could provide important information about past organisms and environments and also may be the key to identifying life on other planets. Scientists have identified what appear to be varnished rocks on the surface of Mars but have not yet been able to bring samples of these rocks back to Earth to test them for trapped life-forms.

References: 13, 103

How do boulders form?

There are three primary ways boulders and boulder fields are created: (1) by mass wasting of unstable slopes, (2) by transport via glaciers or rivers, and (3) by in-place weathering of rock formations. The first, mass wasting of unstable slopes, is basically a fancy way of saying rock fall. Cliff bands and steep mountain faces are typically cracked, the cracks usually resulting from unloading pressure as rocks move from deep in the Earth to its surface. Water and wind exploit these cracks, forming stacks of blocks where competent walls once stood. The blocks eventually succumb to gravity and tumble into talus fields, where the largest of them become boulders. The sandstone bouldering area at Big Bend, near Moab, Utah, is an example of this process. Here large angular blocks of red-colored sandstone fell from the cliffs that border the Colorado River.

Another way boulders form is by the erosive force of glaciers. As glaciers move slowly downhill, they pluck chunks of stone from the surrounding

One common way boulders are formed is by erosion along joint systems, or cracks. This boulder in Vedauwoo, Wyoming, formed by chemical and physical weathering along three perpendicular sets of joints.
PHOTO BY JIM SURETTE

landscape. These stones can range in size from small pebbles to house-size boulders, and they can be plowed along the front and sides of the glacier (the terminal and lateral moraines); or they can move within the ice sheet itself. When the glaciers retreat, the stones are left behind, sometimes ending up hundreds of miles from where they originated. Most of the boulders of New England and the European Alps were formed this way. In fact, many of the swirl-patterned boulders found from Maine to Connecticut are actually chunks of gneiss that originated in Canada.

A third way boulders form is by in-place weathering of large bodies of rock, commonly granite plutons. The boulders and rock formations of Vedauwoo, Wyoming, and Joshua Tree, California, are an example of this process. At Vedauwoo, the 1.4-billion-year-old Sherman granite is eroded preferentially along sets of fractures. The way the fractures are oriented—a set parallel to the ground and a set perpendicular to the ground—results in segmentation of the granite (see figure 20). While the rock is still buried, groundwater invades these fractures, causing chemical weathering and disintegration of the rock. Over geologic time, this process separates the segments of the rock and rounds their edges into smooth boulders (see figure 20).

Why are some boulders blank and some featured?

Why do some boulders have perfectly spaced crimpers on steep walls? Why do other boulders have overhangs riddled with shallow pockets? And why are some boulders completely blank and unclimbable? There is no single answer to any of these questions. The features climbers depend on—features like edges, pockets, and slopers—can develop for a number of different reasons, and these features are *not* developed for just as many reasons. But with a little understanding about rock types, erosive styles, and boulder formation, you can begin to understand the "whys" about your favorite boulder problem.

The features on a boulder depend on a wide variety of factors: rock type, rock fabric, how the boulder formed, how long the boulder has been exposed to weathering. Pockets are common in rock that has been able to dissolve away, like limestone or sandstone cemented by calcite. Pockets are also common in volcanic and volcaniclastic rocks like tuffs and basalts as former air bubbles. Cracks can occur by the fracturing of rocks and by erosion along bedding planes in sedimentary rocks. Edges can be formed anywhere there are textural differences in a rock, including bedding planes, big crystals, flow banding, gneissic banding, foliation, and inclusions.

What determines crystal size?

Why is the granite in Joshua Tree so much coarser than the granite in Yosemite? Why is basalt smooth? The answers to these questions lie in the cooling time of igneous rocks. With igneous rocks—rocks that crystallize from magma—how quickly or slowly the magma cools determines the rock's texture. The slower a magma cools, the more time the crystals have to grow, and the bigger they become. The textural difference between granite and basalt is a good example of this process. Granite is an intrusive igneous rock, meaning that its parent magma cools slowly, beneath the surface of the Earth, leading to the relatively coarse crystals you can see with your naked eye. Basalt, on the other hand, is an extrusive igneous rock, meaning that it forms from magma that erupts on the Earth's surface and is cooled very quickly. Basalt is still made up of individual interlocking crystals, but unlike granite, the crystals are so small that you usually can't see them without a microscope.

Even among intrusive igneous rocks—rocks like granite, diorite, and gabbro—there is significant variation in crystal textures. These variations are due to factors within the crust that influence how long it takes for magma to cool into a rock. Large magma chambers that are deep in the crust will cool more slowly than smaller, shallower magma chambers, for example. Also, the margins of a magma chamber, where they meet the cold host rock (what geologists call the country rock), will tend to cool faster than the interior of the chamber. Another factor is magma composition. The presence of water in a melt, for example, can lengthen the time it takes to cool, thus increasing the size of its crystals.

What makes some granite pink and some gray?

The color of granite comes from the color of its minerals. By definition, granite is made up of quartz, plagioclase (a feldspar with calcium and/or sodium in its structure), and alkali feldspar (a feldspar with potassium in its structure). These are the smoky gray, white, and pink colors of granite. Granite usually also has flecks of black in its palette—crystals of biotite and/or hornblende. If a granite contains a lot of alkali feldspar, it will have a strong pink or even red color. If it contains little alkali feldspar, the granite's overall color will be dominated by the grays and whites of the quartz and plagioclase.

So what makes a granite have more alkali feldspar over plagioclase feldspar, or vice versa? The answer has to do with the chemistry of the magma that formed the granite. The chemistry of the magma has to do with how and where the magma originated in the Earth. Along subduction zones, where oceanic rocks plunge beneath continental rocks, fluids are driven off the oceanic plate, facilitating partial melting of the mantle. This partially melted mantle rises through the continental crust, where it differentiates even more, forming granitic magma chambers and continental volcanoes. The granitic rock of the Sierra Nevada formed this way, as did the rock in the South American Andes. These rocks are typically whitish gray in color because they have more plagioclase feldspar than alkali feldspar. Technically, these rocks are usually classified as granodiorite rather than true granite. On the other hand, where two continents collide, the continental crust becomes thickened. It can get so thick that the deepest rocks—rocks that originated as sediments on the surface of the Earth—become melted. The magma formed from melted sedimentary rocks can form granite with more alkali feldspar than plagioclase feldspar. This is why pink granite is common in places like the Appalachians and the Himalaya.

What is pegmatite, and why is it scary?

Pegmatite is a very coarse-grained, intrusive igneous rock that usually forms dikes that cut across preexisting rock. The important feature of pegmatite is its large grain size: Individual pegmatite crystals can be anywhere between one centimeter and several meters in length. Pegmatite is commonly granitic in composition, containing quartz, plagioclase, and alkali feldspar crystals. Pegmatite can also contain crystals of mica, amphibole (like hornblende), and pyroxene. Pegmatite often forms from the last remaining melt in a magma chamber—melt that can be rich in elements that did not easily crystallize as the magma cooled. These elements, called incompatible elements, can be concentrated enough in pegmatites that rare and even valuable minerals can form. The large grain size in pegmatite is believed to be due to a high water content in the melt, and a specific environment that makes it easier for chemical components to build upon an already nucleated crystal rather than nucleating a new crystal.

Climbers tend to avoid pegmatite because it is chossy. The weakest bonds in a rock are the crystal-to-crystal contacts. If a rock has relatively fine, irregularly shaped crystals, the boundaries of the crystals will make a strong, interlocking network. Think of the hard texture of granite. With very coarse grains, the rock will break along crystal contacts, and because of the coarseness, large crystals will pluck off. The rock has more interfaces for weathering. There are also few natural fractures for putting in gear. So pegmatite is generally difficult to protect and subject to rock fall.

What is basalt? Why does it often form columns?

Basalt is an extrusive igneous rock, meaning it formed from an eruption of lava at or very near the Earth's surface. Basaltic lava flows can have different shapes, depending on how much lava there is, whether it erupts underwater

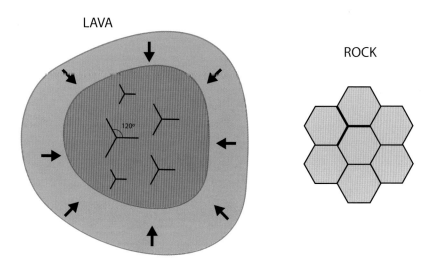

FIGURE 41

Columnar Joints Forming in Volcanic Rocks

This illustration is drawn in map view, or looking down on a surface. As a pool of lava cools, it shrinks, forming cracks in three orientations that intersect at approximately 120 degrees. These cracks coalesce into polygonal columns of hardened volcanic rock, forming the columnar basalts that are common across the American West.

or on dry land, and if it is full of gasses or not. Basalt columns form from a process of cooling and shrinkage in a pool of lava. Cracks form as the lava hardens and shrinks. The cracks are commonly polygonal in form, often hexagonal. This hexagonal shape is due to tensional stresses and the most stable position in terms of surface area. Vertical columns develop because of the direction of heat loss, usually up to the sky and down to the ground. Sometimes the middle of thick lava flows has only weakly formed columns because there the direction of heat loss was not vertical.

Theoretically, shrinkage in a layer of magma or lava, if it is slow and uniform in terms of direction, will form prisms, and the most stable/least amount of energy required is to form three fractures that make 120-degree angles with one another. When these fractures come together, the most stable form is a tessellation of hexagons (see figure 41). In reality, however, shrinkage and cooling is almost never uniform in direction or speed, and thus true hexagons often don't dominate. You can find many pentagons and other forms.

Reference: 11

What are dikes? Why do some have a waffly or blocky appearance?

A dike is an intrusive igneous body that forms a sheet or column that cross-cuts the orientation of the rock it intrudes, which is known as the country rock (see figure 31). Dikes are an important part of the plumbing system of igneous environments in the Earth's crust, transferring magma from deep chambers to the upper parts of volcanoes. The dikes form as magma rises through the crust, creating enough pressure on the surrounding rock that it can fracture. But because the interior of the Earth is under confining pressure, open spaces or voids cannot exist. These fractures instantaneously fill with fluids as they form. In the case of dikes, the fractures fill with magma. Dikes can also form by magma forcing its way through preexisting fractures in the country rock.

Dikes generally cool from the outside inward, like a closing artery. In some dikes, this cooling process is preserved in the form of chilled margins. The quickly quenched magma at the margins of the dike—where it is in contact with the colder country rock—forms very fine-grained igneous rocks. The center of the dike, which stays liquid for longer, has enough time to form larger crystals.

Dikes can be made up of any type of igneous rock. Many dark-colored dikes are basaltic in composition. Dikes of fine-grained granite, called aplite, are also common. Dikes with very large crystals are called pegmatite dikes. It is common to see dikes of different rock type or different texture from the country rock. For example, you can find basaltic dikes cutting across a granitic pluton. Or you can find aplite dikes (very fine-grained granite) cutting across coarse-grained granite. These dikes can form from magma from an adjacent magma chamber that has a different chemistry; or, in the case of the different textures, the magma can come from a different chamber or part of a chamber that has slightly different water content.

Many dikes weather differently from the surrounding rock. In some granitic climbing areas, you can find dikes that are distinctly blocky or waffly in appearance; when viewed up close, these dikes are very fine grained. The blocky textures are formed by sets of joints, or cracks, in the dike that developed during stresses imposed on the rock, possibly during cooling or possibly after cooling by regional forces.

Why are some sandstones white and others red?

The color of sandstones and other sedimentary rock is almost always controlled by iron in the rock. The lack of iron will keep the rock white or beige in color, while the presence of iron can result in colors ranging from green to purple to orange. These different colors have to do with the oxidation state of the iron in the rock. Iron that is formed in an oxidizing environment, which means there is plenty of oxygen, will be red in color, like rust. Iron that is formed in a reducing, or oxygen-poor, environment like deep, anoxic bogs, will be greenish in color.

The color of a sedimentary rock, however, does not necessarily tell you about the environmental conditions of the rock's deposition. The iron in the rock can be part of the rock's cement rather than the grains themselves. Also, the oxidation state of iron in a sedimentary rock can change long after the rock formed. For example, a sediment can be deposited in a reducing environment (oxygen poor), but then fluids can pass through it during cementation and be oxidizing (oxygen rich), changing the iron minerals to a red color.

Zeus, a tower in Canyonlands National Park, is carved out of the bright red sandstone of the Wingate formation.
PHOTO BY JIM SURETTE

What climbing area has the oldest rock? The youngest?

The search for the climbing area with the oldest rock begins by identifying crags and mountain peaks that lie within the ancient cores of the world's continents. These cores are called cratons, and they are the nuclei around which all of the present-day continents were constructed. However, one of the reasons the cratons have survived for billions of years of Earth's history is because they are tectonically very stable, meaning they are also very flat.

Most of the North American Craton, from the northern Midwest of the United States northward across the Canadian Shield, has relatively low relief typical of cratons. The southwest edge of this province, however, is caught up in the mountainous region of Montana and Wyoming. Thus, some of the oldest North American climbing areas lie in the Madison Range of southwest Montana. Here gneisses exposed in the Gallatin Canyon and on Hilgard Peak—two popular spots for climbers—are between 3.3 and 3.5 billion years old, which is approaching the upper limit of the oldest rocks found anywhere on Earth.

Some of the other super-old rocks exposed in this region include the 2.8-billion-year-old Bighorn granodiorite, which makes up some of the northern peaks in Wyoming's Bighorn Mountains. Gannett Peak in the Wind Rivers and Mount Moran in the Teton Range are both approximately 2.7 billion years old. Most of the granitic rocks in the Wind River Range, including the Cirque of the Towers area, are just a bit younger. These are part of the Louis Lake Batholith, which is about 2.6 billion years old. The Grand Teton is made up of Mount Owen quartz monzonite and is about 2.5 billion years old.

Northern Baffin Island is host to rocks in the three-billion-year-old range, but it is unclear if these old rocks are the same as Baffin's climbing destinations. Baffin's Sam Ford Fjord, which has been explored by climbers, exposes quartz- and feldspar-rich granitic gneisses that are about 2.8 billion years old.

There are likely similarly aged or even older climbable rocks in the cores of other continents, especially the ancient continents of Australia and Africa. These areas, however, are less studied and explored by both geologists and climbers.

On the other end of the spectrum, the search for the youngest climbable rock begins with the youngest type of rock that can become competent enough for climbing, which would likely be volcanic in origin. Sedimentary rocks take too long to accumulate and cement; intrusive igneous rocks have

The rock holding up Wyoming's Teton Range is over 2.5 billion years old, making these peaks some of the oldest climbing areas in the world.
PHOTO BY JIM SURETTE

to cool in the Earth's interior and then be uplifted; and metamorphic rocks are almost always going to be old because, by definition, they had an earlier history before metamorphism. Just as we looked in the stable, tectonically quiet cores of the continents to find the oldest rocks, we need to look along the tectonically active, volcanic rims of the continents to find the youngest rocks. This is a tough challenge, as just about anywhere on the so-called "Ring of Fire" around the Pacific Ocean contains young lava flows. Other possible locations are the active plate boundaries of the East African Rift, the Alpine Fault of New Zealand, and the oceanic spreading center in Iceland. Crags made up of volcanic or volcaniclastic rock in any of these locations would top the list of the Earth's youngest climbing areas.

In North America, one of the young climbing areas is Paradise Forks in Arizona. The exact lava flow that forms Paradise Forks has not been dated, but other flows in the same volcanic field are as young as 750 years old. Other North American contenders include Mount Rainier, which is about 500,000 years old. Valles Caldera and some of the tuff crags around Los Alamos, New Mexico, are about one million years old; and the Bishop tuff that makes up Owens River Gorge is 730,000 years old.

References: 30, 51, 52, 72, 93

*Janet Bergman aid climbing
on the Zodiac route, El Capitan.*
PHOTO BY SARAH GARLICK

References

1. Allen, G. M., and Main, M. B. 2005. *Florida's Geological History*. Department of Wildlife Ecology and Conservation Fact Sheet, v. 189.

2. Allmendinger, R. W., and Jordan, T. E. 1997. The Central Andes. *Earth Structure: An Introduction to Structural Geology and Tectonics* (Van der Pluijm, B. A., and Marshak, S., eds.). WCB/McGraw-Hill, p. 430–434.

3. Altenberger, U., Oberhansli, R., Putlitz, B., and Wemmer, K. 2003. Tectonic controls and Cenozoic magmatism at the Torres del Paine, southern Andes (Chile, 51°10′ S). *Revista Geologica de Chile*, v. 30, p. 65–81.

4. Andrichuk, J. M. 1955. Mississippian Madison group stratigraphy and sedimentation in Wyoming and southern Montana. *American Association of Petroleum Geologists Bulletin*, v. 39, p. 2170–2210.

5. Arculus, R. J., and Gust, D. A. 1995. Regional petrology of the San Francisco Volcanic Field, Arizona, USA. *Journal of Petrology*, v. 36, p. 827–861.

6. Baars, D. L. 1993. *Canyonlands Country: Geology of Canyonlands and Arches National Parks*. Salt Lake City: University of Utah Press, p. 138.

7. Baldridge, W. S. 2004. *Geology of the American Southwest: A Journey through Two Billion Years of Plate-Tectonic History*. Cambridge: Cambridge University Press, p. 280.

8. Barker, D. S. 1987. Tertiary alkaline magmatism in Trans-Pecos Texas. Geological Society Special Publications, v. 30, p. 415–431.

9. Barth, A. P., and Wooden, J. L. 2006. Timing of magmatism following initial convergence at a passive margin, southwestern U.S. Cordillera, and ages of lower crustal magma sources. *The Journal of Geology*, v. 114, p. 231–245.

10. Bassett, W. A. 1961. Potassium-argon age of Devils Tower, Wyoming. *Science,* v. 134, p. 1373.

11. Beard, C. N. 1959. Quantitative study of columnar jointing. *Geological Society of America Bulletin,* v. 70, p. 379–382.

12. Becker, T. P., Thomas, W. A., Samson, S. D., and Gehrels, G. E. 2005. Detrital zircon evidence of Laurentian crustal dominance in the lower Pennsylvanian deposits of the Alleghanian clastic wedge in eastern North America. *Sedimentary Geology,* v. 182, p. 59–86.

13. Berardelli, P. 2006. Solving the mystery of desert varnish. *ScienceNow,* July 7, 2006.

14. Bernet, M., Kapoutsos, D., and Bassett, K. 2007. Diagenesis and provenance of Silurian quartz arenites in southeastern New York State. *Sedimentary Geology,* v. 201, p. 43–55.

15. Betts, P. G., Giles, D., Lister, G. S., and Frick, L. R. 2002. Evolution of the Australian lithosphere. *Australian Journal of Earth Sciences,* v. 49, p. 661–695.

16. Bezy, J. V. 2004. A Guide to the Geology of Sabino Canyon and the Catalina Highway. *Down to Earth* (Arizona Geological Survey), v. 17, 45 p.

17. Bosworth, W. 1987. Off-axis volcanism in the Gregory Rift, East Africa: Implications for models of continental rifting. *Geology,* v. 15, p. 397–400.

18. Bothner, W. A., and Loiselle, M. C. 1987. Geology of the Belknap Mountains Complex, White Mountain Series, central New Hampshire. *Geological Society of America Centennial Field Guide—Northeastern Section,* v. 5, p. 263–268.

19. Bradley, D. C., and Hanson, L. S. 2002. Paleocurrent analysis of a deformed Devonian foreland basin in the northern Appalachians, Maine, USA. *Sedimentary Geology,* v. 148, p. 425–447.

20. Bridges, E. M. 1990. *World Geomorphology.* Cambridge: Cambridge University Press.

21. Burchfiel, B. C., Fleck, R. J., Secor, D. T., Vincelette, R. R., and Davis, G. A. 1974. Geology of the Spring Mountains, Nevada. *Geological Society of America Bulletin,* v. 85, p. 1013–1022.

22. Butler, J. R. 1986. Pilot Mountain, North Carolina. *Geological Society of America Centennial Field Guide—Southeastern Section,* p. 227–228.

23. Caldwell, D. W. 1998. *Roadside Geology of Maine*. Missoula: Mountain Press Publishing Company.

24. Cayley, R. A., and Taylor, D. H. 1997. *Grampians Special Map Area Geological Report.* Geological Survey of Victoria Report, v. 107.

25. Chronic, H. 1980. *Roadside Geology of Colorado*. Missoula: Mountain Press Publishing Company, p. 322.

26. Chronic, H. 1983. *Roadside Geology of Arizona*. Missoula: Mountain Press Publishing Company.

27. Churnet, H. G. 1996. Depositional environments of Lower Pennsylvanian coal-bearing siliclastics of southeastern Tennessee, northwestern Georgia, and northeastern Alabama, U.S.A. *International Journal of Coal Geology*, v. 31, p. 21–54.

28. Collins, E. W., and Raney, J. A. 1991. Neotectonic history and geometric segmentation of the Campo Grande Fault: A major structure bounding the Hueco Basin, Trans-Pecos Texas. *Geology*, v. 19, p. 493–496.

29. Coutand, I., Diraison, M., Cobbold, P. R., Gapais, D., Rossello, E. A., and Miller, M. 1999. Structure and kinematics of a foothills transect, Lago Viedma, southern Andes (49°30′ S). *Journal of South American Earth Sciences*, v. 12, p. 1–15.

30. Crumpler, L. S., and Aubele, J. C. 2001. Volcanoes of New Mexico: An abbreviated guide for non-specialists. *Volcanology in New Mexico: New Mexico Museum of Natural History and Science Bulletin*, v. 18: p. 5–15.

31. Curtis, M. L. 2001. Tectonic history of the Ellsworth Mountains, west Antarctica: Reconciling a Gondwana enigma. *Geological Society of America Bulletin*, v. 113, p. 939–958.

32. Dalziel, I., Dalla Salda, L., and Gahagan, L. 1994. Paleozoic Laurentia–Gondwana interaction and the origin of the Appalachian-Andean mountain system. *Geological Society of America Bulletin*, v. 106, p. 243–252.

33. Delaney, P. T. 1987. Ship Rock, New Mexico: The vent of a violent volcanic eruption. *Geological Society of America Centennial Field Guide—Rocky Mountain Section*, p. 411–415.

34. Dever, G. R. J., and Barron, L. S. 1986. Red River Gorge Geological Area (Daniel Boone National Forest) and Natural Bridge State Park, east-central Kentucky. *Geological Society of America Centennial Field Guide—Southeastern Section*, p. 43–46.

35. Dheeradilok, P. 1995. Quaternary coastal morphology and deposition in Thailand. *Quaternary International,* v. 26, p. 49–54.

36. Dorais, M. J. 2003. The petrogenesis and emplacement of the New Hampshire Plutonic Suite. *American Journal of Science,* v. 303, p. 447–487.

37. Dorn, R. I. 2004. Case hardening *Encyclopedia of Geomorphology* (Goudie, A. S., ed.). Routledge, p. 118–119.

38. Drewes, H. 1987. Geologic map and cross-sections of the Dragoon Mountains, southeastern Arizona. U.S. Geological Survey Miscellaneous Investigations Series, I-1662, 2 sheets.

39. Driver, L. A., Creaser, R. A., Chacko, T., and Erdmer, P. 2000. Petrogenesis of the Cretaceous Cassiar Batholith, Yukon–British Columbia, Canada: Implications for magmatism in the North American Cordilleran interior. *Geological Society of America Bulletin,* v. 112, p. 1119–1133.

40. Dyke, C. G., and Dobereiner, L. 1991. Evaluating the strength and deformability of sandstones. *Quarterly Journal of Engineering Geology,* v. 24, p. 123–134.

41. Epstein, J. B. 1993. Stratigraphy of Silurian rocks in Shawangunk Mountain, southeastern New York, including a historical review of nomenclature. *U.S. Geological Survey Bulletin,* v. 1839-L.

42. Eusden, J. D. Jr., Bothner, W. A., and Hussey, A. M. II. 1987. The Kearsarge-Central Maine synclinorium of southeastern New Hampshire and southwestern Maine: Stratigraphic and structural relations of an inverted section. *American Journal of Science,* v. 287, p. 242–264.

43. Eusden, J. D. Jr., Garesche, J. M., Johnson, A. H., Maconochie, J., Peters, S. P., O'Brien, J. B., and Widmann, B. L. 1996. Stratigraphy and ductile structure of the Presidential Range, New Hampshire: Tectonic implications for the Acadian Orogeny. *Geological Society of America Bulletin,* v. 108, p. 417–436.

44. Evans, C. V., and Bothner, W. A. 1993. Genesis of altered Conway Granite (grus) in New Hampshire, USA. *Geoderma,* v. 58, p. 201–218.

45. Evans, J. E., and Reed, J. M. 2007. Integrated loessite-paleokarst depositional system, Early Pennsylvanian Molas Formation, Paradox Basin, southwestern Colorado, USA. *Sedimentary Geology,* v. 195, p. 161–181.

46. Fail, R. T. 1997. A geologic history of the north-central Appalachians, part 2: The Appalachian Basin from the Silurian through the Carboniferous. *American Journal of Science,* v. 297, p. 729–761.

47. Ferris, D. W., and Ferris, M. 2000. "The Geology of Midwestern Rock Climbing Areas," in *Rock Climbing Minnesota and Wisconsin.* Helena: Falcon, p. 13–23.

48. Filer, J. K., and Kleinschmidt, R. F. 1987. The geology of rock climbing. *Mountain State Geology,* p. 10–17.

49. Foster, D. A., and Gray, D. R. 2000. Evolution and structure of the Lachlan Fold Belt (orogen) of eastern Australia. *Annual Review of Earth and Planetary Sciences,* v. 28, p. 47–80.

50. Fraser, J. E., Searle, M. P., Parrish, R. R., and Noble, S. R. 2001. Chronology of deformation, metamorphism, and magmatism in the southern Karakoram Mountains. *Geological Society of America Bulletin,* v. 113, p. 1443–1455.

51. Frost, B. R., Frost, C. D., Cornia, M., Chamberlain, K. R., and Kirkwood, R. 2006. The Teton–Wind River domain: A 2.68–2.67 Ga active margin in the western Wyoming Province. *Canadian Journal of Earth Sciences,* v. 43, p. 1489–1510.

52. Frost, C. D., and Fanning, C. M. 2006. Archean geochronological framework of the Bighorn Mountains, Wyoming. *Canadian Journal of Earth Sciences,* v. 43, p. 1399–1418.

53. Frost, C. D., Frost, B. R., Chamberlain, K. R., and Edwards, B. R. 1999. Petrogenesis of the 1.43-Ga Sherman batholith, SE Wyoming, USA: A reduced, rapakivi-type anorogenic granite. *Journal of Petrology,* v. 40, p. 1771–1802.

54. Goldberg, S. A., and Dallmeyer, R. D. 1997. Chronology of Paleozoic metamorphism and deformation in the Blue Ridge thrust complex, North Carolina and Tennessee. *American Journal of Science,* v. 297, p. 488–526.

55. Greb, S. F., and Chestnut, D. R. Jr. 1996. Lower and lower Middle Pennsylvanian fluvial to estuarine deposition, central Appalachian Basin: Effects of eustasy, tectonics, and climate. *Geological Society of America Bulletin,* v. 108, p. 303–317.

56. Gregory-Wodzicki, K. M. 2000. Uplift history of the central and northern Andes: A review. *Geological Society of America Bulletin,* v. 112, p. 1091–1105.

57. Haddad, S. C., Worden, R. H., Prior, D. J., and Smalley, P. C. 2006. Quartz cement in the Fontainebleau sandstone, Paris Basin, France: Crystallography and implications for mechanisms of cement growth. *Journal of Sedimentary Research,* v. 76, p. 244–256.

58. Hansen, W. R. 1965. The Black Canyon of the Gunnison, today and yesterday. *Geological Survey Bulletin,* v. 1191, p. 76.

59. Hansen, W. R. 1987. The Black Canyon of the Gunnison, Colorado. *Geological Society of America Centennial Field Guide—Rocky Mountain Section,* p. 321–324.

60. Hardeman, W. 1966. Geologic map of Tennessee. Nashville: Tennessee Division of Geology.

61. Harper, S. B. 1999. Morphology of tower karst in Krabi, southern Thailand. *Geological Society of America Abstracts with Programs,* v. 31, p. 52.

62. Harper, S. B. 2002. Mass wasting of coastal headlands in southern Thailand: a comparison. *Geological Society of America Abstracts with Programs,* v. 34, p. 276.

63. Harris, A. G., Tuttle, E., and Tuttle, S. D. 1997. *Geology of National Parks.* Dubuque: Kendall/Hunt Publishing Company.

64. Hatcher, R. D., and Butler, R. J. 1986. Linville Falls Fault at Linville Falls, North Carolina. *Geological Society of America Centennial Field Guide—Southeastern Section,* p. 229–230.

65. Hawkins, A. B., and McConnell, B. J. 1992. Sensitivity of sandstone strength and deformability to changes in moisture content. *Quarterly Journal of Engineering Geology,* v. 25, p. 115–130.

66. Hill, M. 2006. *Geology of the Sierra Nevada.* The University of California Press, 468 p.

67. Hoffman, P. F. 1989. Speculations on Laurentia's first gigayear (2.0 to 1.0 Ga). *Geology,* v. 17, p. 135–138.

68. Horton, B. K., Constenius, K. N., and Decelles, P. G. 2004. Tectonic control on coarse-grained foreland-basin sequences: an example from the Cordilleran foreland basin, Utah. *Geology,* v. 32, p. 637–640.

69. Huber, N. K. 1987. The Geologic Story of Yosemite National Park. *U.S. Geological Society Bulletin,* v. 1595, p. 66.

70. Hudson, M. R. 2000. Coordinated strike-slip and normal faulting in the southern Ozark dome of northern Arkansas: Deformation in a Late Paleozoic foreland. *Geology,* v. 28, p. 511–514.

71. Ingersoll, R. V., Ratajeski, K., Glazner, A. F., and Cloos, M. 1999. Mesozoic convergent margin of central California. California Division of Mines and Geology, Special Publication: *Geologic Field Trips in Northern California,* v. 119.

72. Jackson, G. D., and Berman, R. G. 2000. Precambrian metamorphic and tectonic evolution of northern Baffin Island, Nunavut, Canada. *The Canadian Mineralogist,* v. 38, p. 399–421.

73. Jessup, M. J., Jones, J. V. III, Karlstrom, K. E., Williams, M. L., Connelly, J. N., and Heizler, M. T. 2006. Three Proterozoic orogenic episodes and an intervening exhumation event in the Black Canyon of the Gunnison region, Colorado. *The Journal of Geology,* v. 114, p. 555–576.

74. Keith, S. B., Reynolds, S. J., Damon, P. E., Shafiqulla, M., Livingston, D. E., and Pushkar, P. D. 1980. Evidence for multiple intrusion and deformation within the Santa Catalina-Rincon-Tortolita crystalline complex, southeastern Arizona. *Cordilleran Metamorphic Core Complexes* (Crittenden, M. D., Coney, P. J., and Davis, G. H., eds.). Geological Society of America Memoir, v. 153, p. 217–267.

75. Lanphere, M. A., and Reed, B. L. 1985. The McKinley sequence of granitic rocks: A key element in the accretionary history of southern Alaska. *Journal of Geophysical Research,* v. 90, p. 11413–11430.

76. Lawton, T. F., and Buck, B. J. 2006. Implications of diapir-derived detritus and gypsic paleosols in lower Triassic strata near the Castle Valley salt wall, Paradox Basin, Utah. *Geology,* v. 34, p. 885–888.

77. Lessing, P. 1997. *Geology of the New River Gorge.* West Virginia Geology: Earth Science Studies; www.wvgs.wvnet.edu/www/geology/geoles01 .htm, accessed January 31, 2008.

78. Lever, H. 2007. Review of unconformities in the Late Eocene to Early Miocene successions of the South Island, New Zealand: ages, correlations, and causes. *New Zealand Journal of Geology and Geophysics,* v. 50, p. 245–261.

79. Lillie, R. J. 2005. *Parks and Plates, the Geology of our National Parks, Monuments, and Seashores.* New York: W. W. Norton and Company, 298 p.

80. Love, J. D. 1987. Teton mountain front, Wyoming. *Geological Society of America Centennial Field Guide—Rocky Mountain Section,* p. 173–178.

81. Lyons, J. B., Bothner, W. A., Moench, R. H., and Thompson, J. B. Jr. 1997. Bedrock Geologic Map of New Hampshire. U.S. Geological Survey Special Map, 2 sheets.

82. Maley, T. 1987. *Exploring Idaho Geology.* Boise: Mineral Land Publications, 232 p.

83. McClaughry, J. D., and Ferns, M. L. 2006. Field trip guide to the geology of the lower Crooked River Basin, Redmond and Prineville areas, Oregon. *Oregon Geology,* v. 67, p. 15–23.

84. McDowell, R. C. 1986. The geology of Kentucky: A text to accompany the geologic map of Kentucky. U.S. Geological Survey Professional Paper, v. 1151-H, 76 p.

85. McFarland, J. D. III. 1988. The Paleozoic rocks of the Ponca region, Buffalo National River, Arkansas. *Geological Society of America Centennial Field Guide—South-Central Section,* p. 207–210.

86. McHone, J. G., and Butler, J. R. 1984. Mesozoic igneous provinces of New England and the opening of the North Atlantic Ocean. *Geological Society of America Bulletin,* v. 95, p. 757–765.

87. McKoy, M. L. 1988. Geology of the Seneca Rocks Recreation Area. *Mountain State Geology,* p. 18–28.

88. McNulty, B., and Farber, D. 2002. Active detachment faulting above the Peruvian flat slab. *Geology,* v. 30, p. 567–570.

89. Medaris, L. G. Jr., Singer, B. S., Dott, R. H. Jr., Naymark, A., Johnson, C. M., and Schott, R. C. 2003. Late Paleoproterozoic climate, tectonics and metamorphism in the southern Lake Superior region and proto-North America: evidence from Baraboo interval quartzites. *The Journal of Geology,* v. 111, p. 243–257.

90. Miller, B. V., Fetter, A. H., and Stewart, K. G. 2006. Plutonism in three orogenic pulses, eastern Blue Ridge Province, southern Appalachians. *Geological Society of America Bulletin,* v. 118, p. 171–184.

91. Miller, C. F., Hatcher, R. D. Jr., Ayers, J. C., Coath, C. D., and Harrison, T. M. 2000. Age and zircon inheritance of eastern Blue Ridge plutons, southwestern North Carolina and northeastern Georgia, with implications for magma history and evolution of the southern Appalachian Orogen. *American Journal of Science,* v. 300, p. 142–172.

92. Miller, D. M., and Bedford, D. R. 1999. Pluton intrusion styles, roof subsidence and stoping, and timing of extensional shear zones in the City of Rocks National Reserve, Albion Mountains, southern Idaho. *Geology of Northern Utah and Vicinity (*Spangler, L. E., and Allen, C. J., eds.). Salt Lake City: Utah Geological Association, p. 11–25.

93. Mueller, P. A., Shuster, R. D., Wooden, J. L., Erslev, E. A., and Bowes, D. R. 1993. Age and composition of Archean crystalline rocks from the southern Madison Range, Montana: Implications for crustal evolution in the Wyoming craton. *Geological Society of America Bulletin,* v. 105, p. 437–446.

94. Nicol, A. 1993. Haumurian (c. 66–80 Ma) half-graben development and deformation, mid Waipara, North Canterbury, New Zealand. *New Zealand Journal of Geology and Geophysics,* v. 36, p. 127–130.

95. Oppikofer, T., Jaboyedoff, M., and Keusen, H. R. 2007. High resolution monitoring and analysis of the rock slope collapse of the Eiger (Switzerland). *Geophysical Research Abstracts,* v. 9, p. 03976.

96. Orndorff, R. L. and Futey, D. G. 2007. *Landforms of Southern Utah: A Photographic Exploration.* Missoula: Mountain Press Publishing Company, p. 92.

97. Orr, E. L., Orr, W. N., and Baldwin, W. M. 1992. *Geology of Oregon.* Dubuque: Kendall/Hunt Publishing Company, p. 254 .

98. Osborne, E. W., Szabo, M. W., Neathery, T. L., and Copeland, C. W. Jr. 1988. Geologic Map of Alabama. Geological Society of Alabama Special Map 220.

99. Palais, D. G., and Peacock, S. M. 1990. Metamorphic and stratigraphic constraints on the evolution of the Santa Catalina Mountains metamorphic core complex, Arizona. *Journal of Geophysical Research,* v. 95, p. 501–507.

100. Parrish, R. R., and Tirrul, R. 1989. U-Pb age of the Baltoro Granite, northwest Himalaya, and implications for monazite U-Pb systematics. *Geology,* v. 17, p. 1076–1079.

101. Platt, J. P. 1997. The European Alps, in Van der Pluijm, B. A., and Marshak, S., eds. *Earth Structure: An Introduction to Structural Geology and Tectonics.* WCB/McGraw-Hill, p. 408-415.

102. Price, J. G. 2003. Geology of Nevada, *Betting on Industrial Minerals: Proceedings of the 39th Forum on the Geology of Industrial Minerals* (Castor, S. B., Papke, K. G., and Meeuwig, R. O., eds.). Nevada Bureau of Mines and Geology Special Publication 33.

103. Rakovan, J. 2006. Desert varnish. *Rocks and Minerals,* v. 81, p. 393.

104. Ratajeski, K., Glazner, A. F., and Miller, B. V. 2001. Geology and geochemistry of mafic to felsic plutonic rocks in the Cretaceous Intrusive Suite of Yosemite Valley, California. *Geological Society of America Bulletin,* v. 113, p. 1486–1502.

105. Reed, J. C. Jr. 1964. Geology of the Linville Falls Quadrangle, North Carolina. *U.S. Geological Survey Bulletin,* v. 1161-B.

106. Reid, J. B., Evans, O. C., and Fates, D. G. 1983. Magma mixing in granitic rocks of the central Sierra Nevada, California. *Earth and Planetary Science Letters,* v. 66, p. 243–261.

107. Relmers, P. W., Nelson, B. K., and Nelson, S. W. 1996. Evidence for multiple mechanisms of crustal contamination of magma from compositionally zoned plutons and associated ultramafic intrusions of the Alaska Range. *Journal of Petrology,* v. 37, p. 261–292.

108. Reynolds, S. J. 1988. Geologic Map of Arizona. *Geologic Evolution of Arizona* (Jenney, J. P., and Reynolds, S. J., eds.), v. 17. Tucson: Arizona Geological Society.

109. Rice, C. L. 1984. Sandstone units of the Lee Formation and related strata in eastern Kentucky. U.S. Geological Survey Professional Paper, v. 1151-G, 53 p.

110. Robinson, D. A., and Williams, R. B. G. 2005. Comparative morphology and weathering characteristics of sandstone outcrops in England, UK. *Ferrantia,* v. 44, p. 41–46.

111. Ross, G. M., Patchett, P. J., Hamilton, M., Heaman, L., Decelles, P. G., Rosenberg, E., and Giovanni, M. K. 2005. Evolution of the cordilleran orogen (southwestern Alberta, Canada) inferred from detrital mineral geochronology, geochemistry, and Nd isotopes in the foreland basin. *Geological Society of America Bulletin,* v. 117, p. 747–764.

112. Royden, L. H., and Burchfiel, B. C. 1997. The Tibetan Plateau and Surrounding Regions. *Earth Structure* (van der Pluijm, B. A., and Marshak, S., eds.). WCB/McGraw-Hill, p. 416–423.

113. Schwietering, J. F. 1984. Beneath the New River Gorge. *Mountain State Geology,* v. 84, p. 23–24.

114. Searle, M. P., Simpson, R. L., Law, R. D., Parrish, R. R., and Waters, D. J. 2003. The structural geometry, metamorphic and magmatic evolution of the Everest massif, high Himalaya of Nepal–south Tibet. *Journal of the Geological Society,* London, v. 160, p. 345–366.

115. Selverstone, J., Hodgins, M., Shaw, C., Aleinikoff, J. N., and Fanning, M. C. 1997. Proterozoic tectonics of the northern Colorado Front Range. *Geologic History of the Colorado Front Range,* RMS-AAPG Field Trip #7, p. 8–18.

116. Sharp, R. P., and Glazner, A. F. 1997. *Geology Underfoot: In Death Valley and Owens Valley,* Missoula: Mountain Press Publishing Company.

117. Snoke, A. W. 2005. North America; Southern Cordillera. *Encyclopedia of Geology,* v. 4, p. 48–61.

118. Snoke, A. W. 2006. Personal communication.

119. Spencer, J. E., and Reynolds, S. J. 1989. Middle Tertiary tectonics of Arizona and adjacent areas. *Geologic Evolution of Arizona* (Jenney, J. P., and Reynolds, S. J., eds.), v. 17: Tucson: Arizona Geological Society, p. 539–574.

120. Stewart, K. G., Adams, M. G., and Trupe, C. H. 1997. *Paleozoic Structure, Metamorphism, and Tectonics of the Blue Ridge of Western North Carolina.* Carolina Geological Society Field Trip Guidebook, Carolina Geological Society.

121. Strachan, B. 2007. *Red River Gorge Geology.* Red River Gorge Climbers Coalition Web site: www.rrgcc.org/, accessed January 31, 2007.

122. Sullivan, W. A., and Snoke, A. W. 2007. Comparative anatomy of core-complex development in the northeastern Great Basin, U.S.A. *Rocky Mountain Geology,* v. 42, p. 1–29.

122a. Tabor, R. W., Haugerud, R., and Haugerud, R. A. 1999. *Geology of the North Cascades: A Mountain Mosaic,* Seattle: The Mountaineers Books.

123. Tanaka, K. L., Shoemaker, E. M., Ulrich, G. E., and Wolfe, E. W. 1986. Migration of volcanism in the San Francisco Volcanic Field, Arizona. *Geological Society of America Bulletin*, v. 97, p. 129–141.

124. Turkington, A. V. 1998. Cavernous weathering in sandstone: lessons to be learned from natural exposure. *Quarterly Journal of Engineering Geology*, v. 31, p. 375–383.

125. Turkington, A. V., and Paradise, T. R. 2005. Sandstone weathering: a century of research and innovation. *Geomorphology*, v. 67, p. 229–253.

126. Twidale, C. R., and Vidal Romani, J. R. 2005. *Landforms and Geology of Granite Terrains*. Leiden, A. A.: Balkema Publishers, p. 352.

127. Unrug, R., Ausich, W. I., Bednarczyk, J., Cuffey, R. J., Mamet, B. L., Palmes, S., and Unrug, S. 2000. Paleozoic age of the Walden Creek Group, Ocoee Supergroup, in the Western Blue Ridge, southern Appalachians: implications for evolution of the Appalachian margin of Laurentia. *Geological Society of America Bulletin*, v. 112, p. 982–996.

128. U.S. Geological Survey volcanoes Web site: http://vulcan.wr.usgs.gov/volcanoes/africa/description_africa_volcanics.html, accessed January 31, 2008

129. Van De Kamp, P. C., and Leake, B. E. 1994. Petrology, geochemistry, provenance, and alteration of Pennsylvanian–Permian arkose, Colorado and Utah. *Geological Society of America Bulletin*, v. 105, p. 1571–1582.

130. Van Der Pluijm, B. A., Vrolijk, P. J., Pevear, D. R., Hall, C. M., and Solum, J. 2006. Fault dating in the Canadian Rocky Mountains: evidence for late Cretaceous and early Eocene orogenic pulses. *Geology*, v. 2006, p. 837–840.

131. Veevers, J. J., Cole, D. I., and Cowan, E. J. 1994. Southern Africa: Karoo Basin and Cape Fold Belt. *Permian-Triassic Pangean Basins and Fold Belts along the Panthalassan Margin* (Veevers, J. J., and Powell, C. M. eds.). Geological Society of America Memoir, v. 184, p. 223–280.

132. Vogel, T. A., Cambray, F. W., and Constenius, K. N. 2001. Origin and emplacement of igneous rocks in the central Wasatch mountains, Utah. *Rocky Mountain Geology*, v. 36, p. 119–162.

133. Walker, D., Driese, S. G., and Hatcher, R. D. Jr. 1989. Paleotectonic significance of the quartzite of the Sauratown Mountains window, North Carolina. *Geology*, v. 17, p. 913–917.

134. Walker, D., Simpson, Edward, L., and Driese, Steven G. 1994. Paleogeographic influences on sandstone composition along an evolving passive margin: An example from the basal Chilhowee group (uppermost Proterozoic to lower Cambrian) of the south-central Appalachians. *Journal of Sedimentary Research,* v. A64, p. 807–814.

134a. Whitney, D. L., Tepper, J. H., Hirschmann, M. M., and Hurlow, H. A. 2008. Late orogenic mafic magmatism in the North Cascades, Washington: Petrology and tectonic setting of the Skymo layered intrusion. *Geological Society of America Bulletin,* v. 120, p. 531–542.

135. Wiebe, R. A., Smith, D., Sturm, M., King, E. M., and Seckler, M. S. 1997. Enclaves in the Cadillac mountain granite (coastal Maine): Samples of hybrid magma from the base of the chamber. *Journal of Petrology,* v. 38, p. 393–423.

136. Williams, R., and Robinson, D. 1989. Origin and distribution of polygonal cracking of rock surfaces. *Physical Geography,* v. 71, p. 145–159.

137. Wirth, K., Cordua, W. S., Kean, W. F., Middleton, M., and Naiman, Z. J. 1998. Field trip #2; the geology of the southeastern portion of the Midcontinent Rift System, eastern Minnesota and western Wisconsin. Institute on Lake Superior Geology 44th annual meeting; part 2, field trip guidebook (Boerboom, T. J., and Lusardi, B. A., eds.): p. 166.

138. Witkind, I. J., and Weiss, M. P. 1991. Geologic map of the Nephi 30′ x 60′ quadrangle, Carbon, Emery, Juab, Sanpete, Utah, and Wasatch counties, Utah. IMAP Series, v. I-1937, p. 3 sheets.

139. Wooden, J. L. 2001. Late Cretaceous intrusive migmatites of the Little San Bernardino Mountains, southern California. *American Association of Petroleum Geologists Abstracts,* Cordilleran Section 97th Annual Meeting, April 9–11, 2001.

140. Wyckoff, J. 1999. *Reading the Earth: Landforms in the Making.* Mahway: Adastra West, 352 p.

141. Young, G. M., Minter, W. E. L., and Theron, J. N. 2004. Geochemistry and paleogeography of upper Ordovician glaciogenic sedimentary rocks in the Table Mountain Group, South Africa. *Palaeogeography, Palaeoclimatology, Palaeoecology,* v. 214, p. 323–345.

142. Zachry, D. 2005. Petrographic transition from cratonic to mobile belt provenance, Atoka Formation (Pennsylvanian), northern Arkansas shelf. *Geological Society of America Abstracts with Programs,* v. 37, p. 34.

Index

About the Author

Sarah Garlick has spent over 11 years climbing all types of geologic terrain, from granite big walls and sandstone towers to eroded volcanic necks and glacial erratic boulders. Based in North Conway, New Hampshire, she is the founder and director of Geoscience Outreach, a nonprofit organization that develops science education projects for public audiences. Garlick has a bachelor's degree in geology from Brown University and a master's degree in structural geology and tectonics from the University of Wyoming. She serves as an editor for the scientific journal *Rocky Mountain Geology* and is a contributing writer for major climbing magazines, including *Rock and Ice, Urban Climber,* and *Alpinist.*

Point.
Click.
Send.

Climbing.com